PENGUIN BOOKS

WHAT SPORT TELLS US ABOUT LIFE

'Smith knows his sport, has an eclectic range of sporting references, and his purpose is as much to provoke argument as to answer it. He does it well' *Spectator*

'Educates, informs and entertains' *Daily Telegraph*

'Jaunty and bold . . . he has a clean, epigrammatic style, a flair for aphorism and informed digression. It is a joy to read a professional sportsman who writes so well and has read so widely' *Sunday Telegraph*

'An absolutely delightful book. What Smith says about rhythm in batting is true of writing – poise, balance, etc. – and Smith has it' Simon Gray, author of *The Smoking Diaries*

'I could eat this stuff up with a spoon. The chapter on amateurism is of value to any of us who have managed to end up doing what we love for a living. Smith's entertaining exploration of creativity and inspiration would be every bit as useful to a poet or a songwriter as to an opening batsman' Nick Hornby, *The Believer*

What Sport Tells Us
About Life

ED SMITH

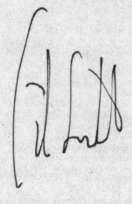

PENGUIN BOOKS

PENGUIN BOOKS

Published by the Penguin Group
Penguin Books Ltd, 80 Strand, London WC2R ORL, England
Penguin Group (USA) Inc., 375 Hudson Street, New York, New York 10014, USA
Penguin Group (Canada), 90 Eglinton Avenue East, Suite 700, Toronto, Ontario, Canada M4P 2Y3
(a division of Pearson Penguin Canada Inc.)
Penguin Ireland, 25 St Stephen's Green, Dublin 2, Ireland (a division of Penguin Books Ltd)
Penguin Group (Australia), 250 Camberwell Road, Camberwell, Victoria 3124, Australia
(a division of Pearson Australia Group Pty Ltd)
Penguin Books India Pvt Ltd, 11 Community Centre, Panchsheel Park, New Delhi – 110 017, India
Penguin Group (NZ), 67 Apollo Drive, Rosedale, North Shore 0632, New Zealand
(a division of Pearson New Zealand Ltd)
Penguin Books (South Africa) (Pty) Ltd, 24 Sturdee Avenue,
Rosebank, Johannesburg 2196, South Africa

Penguin Books Ltd, Registered Offices: 80 Strand, London WC2R ORL, England

www.penguin.com

First published by Viking 2008
Published in Penguin Books 2009

5

Copyright © Ed Smith, 2008

The moral right of the author has been asserted

Beyond a Boundary by C. L. R. James, published by Yellow Jersey Press.
Reprinted by permission of The Random House Group Ltd

Typeset by Rowland Phototypesetting Ltd, Bury St Edmunds, Suffolk
Printed in Great Britain by Clays Ltd, St Ives plc

A CIP catalogue record for this book is available from the British Library

ISBN: 978-0-141-03185-9

www.greenpenguin.co.uk

Penguin Books is committed to a sustainable future
for our business, our readers and our planet.
The book in your hands is made from paper
certified by the Forest Stewardship Council.

For G. M. S.

Contents

Acknowledgements

I am indebted to Andrew Berry, Robert Travers, Mark Williams, Greg Rosenbauer, Nathan Leamon, David Davis, Graeme Gales, Leon Brittan, John Inverarity and Woody Brock for helping me with this book.

Vikram Seth, John Blundell, David Smith, Becky Quintavalle, Jonathan Smith and Beccy Francis read and commented on early drafts of the manuscript.

David Godwin's wisdom and enthusiasm were inspiring throughout this project. Tony Lacey – a polymath about sport and culture – not only often knew a better example but also had the patience to wait until I could see it for myself.

Introduction

What kind of fan are you?

Have you paid a small fortune to be one of 76,000 watching Manchester United at Old Trafford? Or are you a loyal supporter of a tiny team, a bigger cog in an infinitely smaller wheel? Perhaps you are nervously hiding behind a tree, hoping not to convey anxiety to your already panicky son as he gets marooned on 99 in a school cricket match.

What are you doing here? Take your eyes off the pitch for a moment and look around. Glance at the rows of people, whether they are sitting on the recreation park bench or in an international stadium – some may have planned this moment as the centrepiece of their month, others may merely be distracting themselves to avoid weekend boredom. How can one activity – sport – unite such disparate strands of humanity? What on earth have they come to find?

We imagine it is straightforward: everyone sees the same match, even through different eyes. But, in truth, we all have a unique 'take' on sport that means we experience it in an individual way. Perspective is everything.

There is much talk in the sports world about 'experts' and 'mere fans', as though there is an inner caste of privileged insiders who really know what is going on, while the others – the laity – merely gather in the antechapel humming the better hymns. It isn't true. Sports fans of limited knowledge but acute perceptiveness sometimes have far deeper insights about the game than people who are unhealthily obsessed.

The difference between an 'expert' and a 'mere fan' revolves around knowledge – who knows the most. But many of the characteristics which really separate sports fans have nothing to do with degrees of learning. Instead, they derive from differences in temperament. It is temperament that determines how you watch sport, what you see as you do so, which parts of your personality the stuff reaches, how deep it goes and why you come back for more.

One of sport's wonders is the breadth of its support. I use breadth carefully, not meaning simply that lots of people like it – the popularity of sport is well known. Instead I mean the coming together of diametrically differing types of people, all glued to the same pitch or television screen. Some fans love the expectation more than the match itself. Others revel in the spectacle and the sense of theatre. To many supporters, sport is about belonging – to a team, a club or a community of fans. A different type is more detached, imagining himself as the manager or captain, looking down on the mêlée and searching for the right strategy. More common, I expect, is the fan who watches a match like a reader gripped by the narrative of a novel, simply wondering what will happen next.

But there is another huge category of fan: people who just love a bloody good argument. Sport gets them there. It makes them think, engage and argue. Sport stimulates and challenges. It *provokes* them. We know that playing sport is pugilistic; perhaps following sport can be as well.

Sports fans argue about anything and everything. Is too much money bad for sport? Given they've got all these damned statistics, why do they keep picking the wrong team? If the standard of sport is supposed to be improving, why do today's players seem less good than yesterday's giants? What part does luck play in top-class sport? How could anyone lose his cool in his swansong? What still motivates someone who has already won everything? Does what happened last season influence the next? How can we get out of this mess?

Unravel the ideas behind the arguments in those few sentences and you will find questions about evolution, destiny, psychology, the free market, history and many other disciplines.

That might sound daunting, but it should be liberating. Sport can be enjoyed at lots of different levels – just like music, literature or art. You don't have to take an intellectual or analytical approach to love it. If you turn the pages of the novel simply to find out what happens next you are still getting your money's worth. But potentially there is also a deeper level of enjoyment.

So it is with sport. I am not arguing that you should care more about sport in the conventional sense of sitting for *even* longer with your head in your hands while your team crashes to defeat. In many ways we already take it more than earnestly enough. But given that people already take sport so very seriously, and at such an intense level of enquiry, then we might as well draw out some of sport's intellectual lessons and practical uses while we're arguing about it. Sport, I think, is a huge and mostly unused analytical resource. This book tries to explore that resource.

Sport has a rich conceptual framework, if only we would open our eyes to it. If you want to prove how much luck intervenes in history, sport is the perfect place to start the enquiry. If you want to know how to change an institution, sport has great examples. Sport pits nature against nurture and lets us all watch and take sides. If you wonder about the limits of objectivity, sport raises the question of the relationship between facts and opinion. Sport invites nostalgia about a mythic golden age, then mocks it by holding up a stopwatch that shows ever-improving world-record times.

We see what we want to see when we watch sport. The angry fan finds tribal belonging; the pessimist sees steady decline and fall; the optimist hails progress in each innovation; the sympathetic soul feels every blow and disappointment; the rationalist wonders how the haze of illogical thinking endures.

From the players and the fans to the institutions and the record books, sport is full of statistics, prejudices, perspectives and historical changes – the unavoidable stuff of life. Most of these chapters start with a simple question about one sporting issue, and then expand and connect it to the outside world. Sport is a condensed version of life – only it matters less and comes up with better statistics. Consequently, in this book, I place sport in the widest possible context in order to learn more about the game of real life.

More importantly, I hope this book may spark many new arguments, provoke disagreement from many quarters, and perhaps even resolve the odd existing row.

1. Why there will never be another Bradman

Sport appeals equally to two apparently contradictory world-views. First, the notion of a golden age of true heroes from which we have gradually declined. Second, the evolutionary view of human progress that sees sport as perpetually improving. Which is right? Or is there some way that both theories can be true?

To begin with, we should at least try to be objective and look at sports that are easily and precisely measured, like athletics. Where scientific tools are available to us, do they show sport to be getting better?

Until Roger Bannister managed it in 1954, many thought that running a mile in under four minutes was impossible. As one contemporary writer explained, the figure 'seemed so perfectly round – four laps, four quarter miles, four-point-o-o minutes – that it seemed God had established it as man's limit'. One of the most revered athletics coaches, Brutus Hamilton, agreed. He published 'The Ultimate of Human Effort', which stated that the quickest mile ever possible was 4:01.6. Anything faster than that was beyond human capacity. Some even thought that running that fast was dangerous, perhaps lethal. 'How did he know he would not die?' a Frenchman asked about Bannister afterwards.

The point isn't that Bannister famously broke the four-minute 'barrier' on the Iffley Road track in Oxford on 6 May 1954. These days, four minutes isn't even a landmark, let alone a barrier. The current record, 3:43.13 – held by Hicham El Guerrouj – is more than 7 per cent faster than Bannister's speed. The four-minute mile was not a God-given barrier at all, just another step in human evolution. Marathon running makes the point even more starkly. In 1896 it took the Olympic gold medallist just under three hours. Now the best marathon runners hover around the two-hour mark.

There are all sorts of reasons for the sharp increase in human athletic evolution. First, modern training is far more scientific and advanced. Secondly, the professionalization of sport means that athletes can devote their entire lives to improvement. (Bannister, on the other hand, squeezed his training into hour-long lunchtime breaks from his medical studies. He couldn't even take the day off after breaking the four-minute mile – and turned up as normal to St Mary's Hospital, Paddington.) Thirdly, nutritionists fine-tune athletes' diets to make sure they will be in perfect physical condition come race day.

Tactics and techniques have also advanced, sometimes, quite literally, in huge jumps. In the case of the Fosbury flop, one jump changed everything. Before 1968, high-jumpers took off from their inside foot and swung their outside foot up and over the bar. But at the 1968 Mexico City Olympics, an American, Dick Fosbury, raced up to the bar at great speed and took off from his right (outside) foot. Then he twisted his body, going over the bar head first, but with his back facing down. The world's coaches shook their heads in disbelief. Fosbury jumped 2.24 metres and won gold. By 1980, thirteen of the sixteen Olympic finalists were using the Fosbury flop. The world record – by Fosbury flop, of course – now stands at 2.45 metres.

A similar innovation was made in the shot-put by Parry O'Brien, who – just two days after Bannister broke the four-minute mile – became the first man to put the shot more than sixty feet, a barrier thought to be almost as unbreakable. Where putters had previously rocked back and forth, then hopped across the shot-put circle to their throw, O'Brien turned his back to the landing area, then spun 180 degrees, gliding across the circle before releasing. It worked. He set his first world record in 1953, and went on to break it sixteen times.

Deeper longer-term demographic trends have also helped records tumble. Most sportsmen are naturally bigger and stronger than their ancestors, even before stepping onto a training field. A twelve-year-old child in 1990 (who was in what the World Health Organization calls 'average economic circumstances') was about nine inches taller than his 1900 counterpart. Improved diet and health have made us grow bigger and grow up earlier. More obviously, worldwide population has exploded, so the talent pool of potential record-breakers has increased hugely. You are far more likely to find someone who can run a four-minute mile in a sample of several million perfectly healthy people than in a sample, say, of only 10,000.

So, if health care becomes increasingly available around the world; and diet continues to improve; and training techniques become more scientific – then surely sporting aptitude will continue to evolve indefinitely? In which case, won't each generation of athletes be fully justified in looking back on the last bunch of weaklings and laughing at them?

No. There are some barriers that simply cannot be broken. 'We will never run a mile at the same speed at which we now run 100 metres,' as the Harvard evolutionary geneticist Andrew Berry has explained. 'The laws of oxygen exchange will not permit it.'

Racehorses seem already to have reached that physical limit. Like human athletes, for years their speed records steadily improved. From 1850 to 1930, the winning times for the Derby dropped from 2:55 to 2:39. But then horses simply stopped getting faster. From 1986 to 1996, the average time stayed at 2:39. Racehorses, unlike humans (so far as I know), are specifically bred to run. The stud industry seeks to preserve the best genes and match them with perfect partners. So generations of professional genetic selection have ensured that today's elite racehorse has every conceivable speed characteristic. But you can only go so far. You can only breed horses with ultralight thin bones to a particular point; the bones will crack under stress if they get any lighter.

The same principles will one day apply to humans. 'Human improvement,' Berry concluded, 'must eventually bow to the basic constraints of biomechanics.' There is indeed an outer-wall of human endeavour. It is just that no one knows where it is. But we do know it isn't the four-minute mile. Evolution has a good way to run yet.

There is an obvious difficulty in applying this scientific method of measurement to other sports. Cricket, for example, is a predominantly skill game – it pits bat against ball, and neither against a constant clock. There is also the Bradman problem: cricket's towering achiever played from 1928 to 1948, and in half a century of professional cricket – for all the new training, better diets and vast talent pool – no one has got anywhere near him. How's that for human evolution?

In fact, the Bradman problem is not unique to cricket. Being outstanding seems to be getting harder. In baseball, the holy grail for batters is to average over .400. No one has actually done that since Ted Williams in 1941 – but if you look at the fifty years before then, eight players managed even better and hit .410. The same is true for cricket. According to the *Wisden Book of Test Cricket*, twelve English batsmen born before the First World War had an average of above 50; an achievement matched by only three players born after it.

This is the central paradox of sporting progress. If the standard of sport is generally improving, why do the greats of the past stand out more? Three reasons: better defence, more information and a higher base level of achievement.

The first thing a coach can do in any sport is to provide a defensive structure. Attack and flair, which rely more on instinct, are harder to systematize. But defence is more a question of alignment and tactics – which means that even quite a small degree of thinking and planning can make a big difference.

I notice this during practice routines on match days and on training days. About ninety minutes before play starts, many professional cricket teams split into two groups and play a game of touch-rugby as a physical warm-up. Obviously, if you end up with too many of the natural athletes on one team, that side is going to win. But given two roughly balanced teams, if one of them takes defence at all seriously – tracks back, lines up properly, counts opposing players – it can easily make scoring very difficult for the opposition. (My own role in this defensive machine, as my team-mates at Middlesex will attest, is not always as central as it might be.) Usually, no one can be bothered to do much more than enjoy a bit of competitiveness and self-expression, and one side wins by default. But a defensive stalemate is quite easily achieved when both sides take defence seriously.

The organization–defence principle applies equally in other sports. An American friend once persuaded me to play football in a casual round-robin competition one Sunday in New York's Central Park. (He made the mistake of thinking that as I was a cricketer I must have some footballing skill too.) I was hopeless, the team of Brazilians were brilliant, and our team spent most of the day watching from the sidelines. It was immediately obvious that although no amount of coaching or tactics would ever reverse the result – the Brazilians would always be the best, our team would always be one of the weaker sides – some more organization and coaching would reduce the margin of defeat. A really thorough defensive plan might help us to lose merely 2–0 or 1–0 instead of 4–0. (*Why* anyone would bother to even think about losing 'better' on a sunny Sunday in the park is a very good question.)

But the broader point applies to spheres which do matter. Defensive errors in all sports are often the result of bad planning and organization. Improve the 'systems' for every team in any given league and the result is not more goals, but fewer goals: defences are harder to break down and teams bunch up in terms of scoring. The good teams, in other words, stand out less obviously.

Secondly, professional sports teams now have much better information about the opposition. Access to television footage, newspapers, books and the internet all means that you can analyse future opponents in huge detail. Steve Waugh used to say that reading autobiographies was a great way to discover revealing weaknesses in current opposing players. In general, more is known about everyone in modern professional sport than ever before – and, as a result, more strategies are devised to counteract exceptional players.

Again, the easiest application of all that information is defensive. The Bodyline theory was infamously devised to stop Bradman. Bodyline may have been extreme and unusually unsporting, but it was philosophically ahead of its time. These days, devising strategies to limit opposing star players is commonplace – bowling well wide of Tendulkar's off-stump, for example. More to the point, having endless footage of opposing players on tape removes an element of subjectivity from strategic planning. It is simply a fact where next week's opposing opener scores his runs – a Sky Sports wagon-wheel, the graphic which demonstrates each batsman's scoring distribution, proves the point.

Thirdly, the less good players in professional sport are a lot better than they used to be. The scientist, polymath and baseball nut Stephen Jay Gould did a study of the history of baseball averages. He found that as the game improved, the lowest averages crept up. An average that once made you a struggling but employed baseball player, now leaves you out of a job. And yet the overall batting average has remained reasonably constant. In fact, there is exact symmetry – as the worst have got better, the best have stood out less. As we have already seen, no one hits .400 any more.

Gould explained all this as a perfect scientific example of 'declining variation' – the bunching of elite sportsmen as the professional league improves overall. In an article for *Vanity Fair*, Gould measured this decline in variation throughout the history of major league baseball. He simply took the five highest and five lowest averages in each season and compared them to the league average. He discovered that 'the differences between both average and highest and between average and lowest have decreased steadily through the years.'

Gould's proper science provides the maths to back up my unproven park-soccer intuition. He was surely right in his conclusion that '*Systems equilibriate as they improve.*' He argued, therefore, that 'the extinction of .400 hitting is, paradoxically, a mark of increasingly better play.'

Later, unhappy with the coarseness of his statistical sample, he nailed his case about the declining variety of batting averages even more firmly. Gould explained his method as follows:

The standard deviation is a statistician's basic measure of variation. To compute the standard deviation, you take each individual batting average and subtract it from the league average for that year. You then square each value in order to eliminate negative numbers for batting averages below the mean (a negative times a negative gives a positive number). You then add up all these values and divide them by the total number of players – giving an average squared deviation of individual players from the mean. Finally, you take the square root of this number to obtain the average, or standard, deviation itself.

Well, exactly – I couldn't have put it better myself.

Answer – 'Our hypothesis is clearly confirmed. Standard deviations have been dropping steadily and irreversibly.' In layman's terms: as play improves overall, the gap between best and worst narrows.

In a cricketing context, Gould's argument provides a scientific explanation of why there will never be another Bradman, even – in fact, *especially* – if the standard of general play does constantly improve. The sophistication of the modern game works against freakish solo domination. In skill-centred sports rather than purely physical sports, some records really are unbreakable.

The case of Bradman, in fact, proves Gould's point better than any baseball player could. Bradman was better at cricket than anyone has ever been at any other measurable sport. His feats are more remarkable, the second-best player is further adrift, the chasing pack trails by a greater margin. When Bradman died in February 2001, the *New York Times* mathematically converted his cricket average into other sporting measures – basketball points per game, baseball hits per inning. Bradman, they concluded, was better than Michael Jordan or Babe Ruth or Ty Cobb.

A group of cricket statisticians, following Gould's methods, undertook an analysis of all Test batsmen between 1877 and 1997. By plotting the coefficient of variation of batting averages across eras, they showed that variability had decreased over time. For a current player to be relatively as 'good' as Bradman – factoring in the greater 'bunching' of today's great players – you would need to average about 77. No one is yet out of the high 50s. Bradman remains the greatest of the giants of sport's golden age.

When I was five and he was seventy-three, I met Sir Donald Bradman in Adelaide. It was the Smiths' first big family holiday, and in South Australia we stayed with friends who lived two doors along from the great man. I was already crazy about cricket, and our friends kindly arranged for us all to have tea with the Don and for me to have a net session in the back garden.

So, I was to bat in front of the Don. It was the ultimate dream come true for a cricket-mad kid. I was old enough to be thrilled, but young enough (thankfully) not to be burdened by understanding quite how astonishingly lucky I was. I spent most days hitting cricket balls anyway – I would hang a ball in a sock and tie it from a tree like a pendulum so I could hit as many balls as I liked. The scheduled net session just promised a better audience.

The big day arrived – a warm, sunny afternoon in the Australian winter. I remember meeting a shrewd-looking old man who seemed to have a sharp, analytical expression. A few balls were thrown for me to hit into a net. He watched and didn't say much. More balls were thrown. I hit some okay with my beloved size 3 Stuart Surridge cricket bat.

'For God's sake, stop throwing him half-volleys – make it a bit harder for the lad!' he exclaimed. The Don had spoken and everyone laughed.

I didn't realize then, of course, what writing this has helped me understand now. I had been privileged to meet not only a genius – there will always be geniuses – but a genius from an age when they stood taller above their contemporaries. The sporting world was smaller in Bradman's time, so its giants loomed larger. No one stood higher than him.

There truly was a time when great men were greater – but human progress means those days will never come back. There really will never be another Bradman.

2. The age of the amateur has passed. Worse luck

Beware false dualities: classical and romantic, real and ideal, reason and instinct . . . Dualities which are defined at the same moment (stoic and epicurean, Whig and Tory) become united by the historical process, and end by having more, not less, in common . . . Ideas which have for long divided individuals will become meaningless in the light of the forces that will separate groups.

The river of truth is always splitting up into arms that reunite. Islanded between them the inhabitants argue for a lifetime as to which is the mainland

– Cyril Connolly, *The Unquiet Grave*

One generation's favourite idea is despised by the next as old-fashioned rubbish. That is what has happened to amateurism.

At its peak, the character-building philosophy of amateurism defined British attitudes to sport. A century ago 'amateur' was a compliment to someone who played sport simply for the love of it – it is derived, after all, from the Latin for 'to love'. The word professional, on the other hand, scarcely existed as a noun.

How the wheel has turned. In fact, the words have almost completely swapped meanings. 'Professional' now has a definition so broad that almost anyone who has held down a job for a few months can call himself a 'true professional'. And amateurism has become a byword for sloppiness, disorganization and ineptitude.

'The amateur, formerly the symbol of fair play and a stout heart,' as the literary critic D. J. Taylor put it, 'became the watchword for terminal second-rateness and lower-rung incompetence.' Have we thrown out the baby with the bathwater?

There is no doubt that the survival of amateur rhetoric so far into the twentieth century was a bizarre anachronism, even by British standards. When Fred Titmus made his debut for Middlesex in 1949, his progress to the wicket was accompanied by a loudspeaker announcement correcting an error on the score-card: 'F. J. Titmus should, of course, read Titmus, F. J.' A gentleman was allowed his initials before the surname; a professional's came after. People felt these things mattered.

There are countless stories about grand but hopeless amateurs insisting that far more talented pros called them 'Mr' – even on the field of play. Right up until the 1970s, any MCC member – even one who could scarcely hold a bat let alone play first-class cricket – had the right to demand that the MCC young professionals bowled at him in the Lord's nets.

Clearly the amateur ideal – in its snobbery, exclusivity

and sometimes plain silliness – assisted in its own demise. But now professionalism has had a good crack of the whip, perhaps it is time we drew stock about where that idea has taken us. And as we wave amateurism goodbye, could there be anything in its wreckage that might be worth salvaging?

First of all, we might consider whether amateurism allowed for a broad church of personalities, and encouraged an instinctiveness and individuality that is well suited to producing success in sport. Secondly, perhaps amateurism left people alone more – and it might be that great players respond well to being left alone.

It is a truism that there is a creative element to the best sport. We crave creative midfield footballers, creative managers and creative leadership. Alongside their creativity, sportsmen are often lauded when they seem inspired – we talk of an inspired spell of bowling, an inspired tactical move or an inspirational act of defiance. The language of sporting excellence draws heavily from the arts – for the very good reason that playing sport has much in common with artistic expression.

What do we mean when we talk of creativity and inspiration? Perhaps we can never fully understand the answer. Many of the most inspired sporting achievements, like great works of art or innovation, spring from parts of our personalities which resist rational analysis, let alone professional planning. Where does a writer find inspiration for a novel? Where do scientific ideas come from, how does an entrepreneur come up with a new business idea? There will be an element of self-awareness in all these processes – a management of talent, a regulation of originality

– but also a good amount of instinct. Forces beyond rationality lead creative people to follow certain paths and not others. Like strikers with an instinct for where to be in the penalty area, something takes them into different (and better) creative territory.

Crucially, the wisest of these original minds know better than to over-analyse the sources of their inspiration. They do not undermine the muse by trying to master her. Whatever works should be left well alone. 'If the word "inspiration" is to have any meaning,' wrote T. S. Eliot, 'it must mean that the speaker or writer is uttering something which he does not wholly understand – or which he may even misinterpret when the inspiration has departed from him.' After all, 'inspiration' derives linguistically from the concept of breath – once breathed out, it is gone.

Bob Dylan has argued that inspiration needs to be protected from too much 'grown-up' self-analysis: 'As you get older, you get smarter and that can hinder you because you try to gain control over the creative impulse.' Many sportsmen, in the same way, succeed not *despite* inexperience, but *because* of it. Experience brings wisdom to some, but over-analysis to most. Sometimes, we simply learn new impediments to creative self-expression. You've got to unlearn them.

'Creativity is not like a freight train going down the tracks,' Dylan writes in his autobiography, *Chronicles*. 'It's something that has to be caressed and treated with a great deal of respect. If your mind is intellectually in the way, it will stop you. You've got to programme your brain not to think too much.'

Programme your brain not to think too much? A typical

Dylan paradox, but one that makes perfect sense. Learning to be better at creativity or self-expression, in other words, has much to do with unlearning inhibiting forms of cleverness. Dylan, following his own advice, undercut the claims people made about his genius. 'Just a song and dance man,' he said.

Few of us doubt that inspiration and creativity have much to do with sporting excellence as well as artistic experience. And yet the sporting world is increasingly reluctant to leave sporting inspiration alone, as Dylan and Eliot recommend. That is because professionalism tends to encourage sportsmen to examine *how* – at a conscious level – they play at their best.

The sportswriter Simon Barnes, perhaps alluding to his own literary talent as well as the athletic gifts of the sportsmen he has spent his lifetime studying, has questioned the wisdom of this strand of professionalism. 'If you look at your own talent too searchingly, it might cease to be what it is. If you bring these highly trained but deeply instinctual matters to the level of conscious thought, the magic stuff might never happen again . . . Ian Botham would only describe his outbursts of brilliance with the phrase "it sort of clicks".'

This leads back to the arts. As the literary critic Christopher Ricks put it: 'An artist is someone more than usually blessed with a cooperative subconscious, more than usually able to effect things with the help of instincts and intuitions of which he or she is not necessarily conscious. Like the great athlete, the great artist is at once highly trained and deeply instinctual.'

Inspiration, in other words, implies an alignment of

conscious and subconscious living. So how do you achieve this 'cooperative subconscious'? As that question is about self-expression and the creative journey, it can never be answered twice in the same way. We may as well ask, how do you become original? The 'answer' is by living originally.

But I fear future generations of sportsmen will be encouraged to find trite answers to these profound questions. Ours is the age of psychoanalysis, and it has given names to things that sportsmen might be better off leaving undefined. Sport has fallen victim to the cult of self-improvement via self-discovery – it is the foundation on which much sports psychology is built. Above all, professionalism (unlike amateurism) likes to think it is *in control* – that it has got a work ethic, a clear process and a precise system. Without mastery over inspiration, professionalism struggles to justify the big wage bills. But in truth, no one can master inspiration – that is its definition. You can only mess it up.

So although a degree of self-awareness may be necessary, even useful, the journey of self-analysis can be taken too far. We shouldn't psychoanalyse inspiration – because it doesn't like to be in the psychiatrist's chair. Physical genius often depends on an element of mystery.

If someone has got something special, it is often the best idea to leave him well alone. Hence the irony of professionalism is that so much organization and time is dedicated to understanding and improving something which is sometimes beyond meddling interference: self-expression and instinct. To over-clarify that realm may serve to domesticate and disempower it.

So I would argue there is also a pragmatic reason for retaining a splash of the amateur spirit: it is often a big part of how victories happen. One half of sport may be about harnessing human talent, but the other half depends on setting it free. In that sense, sport is just like other forms of self-expression.

A sports fan might object to likening sport to artistic creativity on the grounds that sport is outcome-based. We're not after an interesting end result. We're after *a result* – full stop. In retrospect, we might say it's all about the journey, but at the time it is the points that seem really important. The artists can travel freestyle all they want, but we practical performers need a professional road map.

Except often there isn't one. Even the most professional worlds have their blind spots – and those moments are often the most important. Take medicine, a profession that is far more scientific than sport – and where the outcome can be a matter of life and death. It would be reassuring, if we ever had to face major surgery, to think that all eventualities were covered, that science had written the book, that human instinct didn't come into it, that decades of professional medicine had come up with a cast-iron procedure. No room for any amateurishness here, right?

But we would be wrong. In a *New Yorker* profile of Charlie Wilson, one of America's most brilliant neuro-surgeons, he explained the role of 'feel' and intuition in brain surgery:

Sometimes during the course of an operation, there'll be several possible ways of doing something, and I'll size them up and, without having any conscious reason, I'll just do one of them

. . . It's sort of an invisible hand. It begins to feel almost mystical. Sometimes a resident asks, 'Why did you do that?' and I say, 'Well, it just seemed like the right thing.'

Understanding this requires us to hold together two ideas that professionalism often presents as contradictory: expertise and instinctive decision-making. The former does not negate the need for the latter. The two are co-dependent.

If it's good enough for Charlie Wilson . . .

From neurosurgery to Wayne Rooney. After England's lacklustre victory over Trinidad and Tobago in the 2006 World Cup, Simon Barnes – revisiting the ideas behind his comments about Ian Botham – wrote an unusual article about Felipe Scolari, amateurism and Wayne Rooney. (A sequence of words not often found in the same sentence.) Scolari, who managed Brazil to the 2002 World Cup, is so well respected that he is sometimes happy to say what he thinks, not what he imagines people want to hear.

Scolari said: 'My priority is to ensure that players feel more amateur than professional. Thirty to forty years ago, the effort was the other way. Now there is so much professionalism, we have to revert to urging players to like the game, love it, do it with joy.'

This is not romantic twaddle. It is a fact that the more important something gets, the harder it is to do it well. We can all walk along a kerbstone in safety: but if the drop were not six inches but six miles, how then would we walk? Football matters too much; it matters to the players too much. As a result, the mattering gets in the way of the playing . . .

. . . [the great sportsman is often] the person who can free himself from the straitjacket of professional concern and play the damn ball without thinking about it too hard. And if he can do so with joy, so much the better.

For Rooney, the drop from the kerbstone was only six inches: he played as if falling were nothing. David Moyes, his former manager at Everton, called Rooney 'the last of the back-street footballers', and that was how Rooney looked from the first minute he began playing football in his first World Cup finals. And the truly remarkable thing was that Rooney's joyful attitude infected everybody else in the team. In an instant England switched from careworn to carefree; and as a result, two goals were scored and England are through to the round of sixteen.

Reading that reminded me about the arrival on the international stage of another immensely talented and entertaining sportsman – Kevin Pietersen. Like Rooney, Pietersen seems naturally not to worry about the consequences of his play. The negatives – what if I make a huge error, or precipitate defeat, or look ridiculous? – don't creep into his mind. 'Whatever will be, will be,' Pietersen is fond of saying – the explanation, he believes, for why he has 'absolutely no fear of failure'.

Though both Pietersen and Rooney are instinctively carefree, that has nothing to do with not caring – I am sure they both care a great deal. But the caring doesn't get in the way of the performing, as it seems to for so many sportsmen who try to find their best on the big stage.

I know Pietersen as an opponent and team-mate. We were both on the England 'A' tour to India in 2003/4, which put him firmly in the England selectors' minds, and

I remember how unbothered he was about lots of issues that seemed to weigh down other players. He never gave the impression of being concerned about what the coaches or selectors thought about him. He just played, and he played very well indeed.

Geoff Boycott, a great fan of Pietersen's, has likened him to Denis Compton, batting genius and Brylcreem poster boy of the 1940s and '50s. How ironic that a native South African should have inherited the mantle of that most dashing and English of heroes. Perhaps a generation of modern English professionals, brought up to believe that all aspects of amateurism were 'amateurish' and defeatist, spent too much energy thinking about what they should *not* be doing – and so lost some of their instinctiveness and sense of joy. Avoiding the tenets of amateurism, after all, certainly does not make you a good professional.

It is revealing to look at the opposite of Kevin Pietersen, someone whose obvious brilliance was never given full voice on the international stage – Mark Ramprakash. The story of Ramprakash's 'unfulfilled talent' has become a journalistic staple, so great is the shortfall between his first-class record and his Test average.

In the ten years I have been playing county cricket, more dressing-room hours have been spent discussing his career than any other. Even a tough judge like Justin Langer has expressed incredulity that Ramprakash didn't 'convert' at Test level. How could Ramprakash be so talented and so technically adept and yet not come through eventually? Did he lack run-scoring options against certain bowlers? Was he so concerned with not 'giving his wicket away' that he ended up getting out too often in the 'right' way (i.e.

nicking good balls)? Was he dropped from the England team so many times that it became impossible for him not to be constantly looking over his shoulder? Did he try too hard?

The Australian Michael Bevan, who was equally talented and prolific – Bevan himself, though he became the best one-day player in the world, perhaps never fulfilled himself in Tests – probably got closest to understanding the Ramprakash question. 'He probably just took the whole thing too seriously – that's easily done in Test cricket.'

No career as prolific as Ramprakash's, no matter what its frustrations, should ever be discussed exclusively in negative terms. For nearly two decades, he has been a master batsman in first-class cricket – respected by his team-mates and feared by opponents. Ramprakash, in an interview with former teammate Simon Hughes, has argued that the disappointing pattern of his Test career owed much to an overly 'professional' outlook:

When I was eighteen cricket was a game. I used to go in and try to hit Malcolm Marshall over the top. Then it became a job as I became more seasoned and expected to perform. People look to you to produce. From the age of twenty-one I started every season thinking if I play well, I could play Test cricket. I put pressure on myself. But there were a lot of people with one Test cap. The axe could fall at any time. It was really tough. More recently I've realized I hadn't enjoyed the game as much as I would have liked and so I've been determined to enjoy the game more.

It seems to have been working. In 2006, the thirty-seven-year-old Ramprakash made an astonishing 2,278 runs for Surrey, making him only the sixth batsman in history to finish the English summer with an average of over 100. In 2007, he did it again – an unprecedented consecutive double.

As if to underline his new-found freedom, in the off-season Ramprakash agreed to appear in the TV series *Strictly Come Dancing*:

Every session was so enthusiastic, varied and fun – it's an attitude that could really make a crossover to cricket. Cricket practice can be so technical and stereotyped. Everyone's so worried about the left elbow – is it in the right place? Cricket's a game! Something to be enjoyed. That would be one massive thing I've got from this.

A splash of amateurism had entered his life and his game. Certainly, no one is better placed than Ramprakash to understand how important it is to escape the straitjacket of an over-professional mindset.

Angst, it seems, rarely works. If you deviate too far from a straightforward outlook of 'I've done the hard work in planning and practice, now I'm just going to play', trouble is usually just around the corner. Playing at your best in sport has a lot to do with finding your true 'voice' as a player, and it helps if that voice is as simple and natural as it can be.

All professional sportsmen battle with their fears and anxieties. And by no means do they always conquer them. We live on the brink – of disappointment, of failure, of being dropped, of getting sacked, of retreating back into civilian life with our dreams unfulfilled. That is the parlous state in which most sportsmen usually find themselves. All of us have experienced downward spirals of anxiety and introspection – I am losing form, my place is in jeopardy, my career could be in danger. Often you deny the problem, which secretly increases your anxiety – you are scared of admitting your fears even to yourself – and your form worsens still further.

Eventually – better players do this earlier and more efficiently than others – there is a moment of acceptance: I *am* playing under-par, maybe I am in danger of being dropped, perhaps I do need a score to survive. Now what? Admitting those facts doesn't actually change anything. You have only to do one thing to solve all those problems: play well. Just play well. Don't let anything come between you and playing well. Remove the obstacles to playing well. Anxiety is one of the obstacles. Worrying is one of the obstacles. Thinking too far ahead of yourself is one of the obstacles. Not playing in the now is one of the obstacles. Failing to focus simply and only on the job in hand is one of the obstacles. Getting sport out of proportion is one of the obstacles. Believing your life and your struggle to be disproportionately important is one of the obstacles. Dreading failure is one of the obstacles.

Now you are thinking like a player again. That is usually the beginning of a return to form.

For the vast majority – all except the Pietersens and the Rooneys – it is a question of reaching an *accommodation* with the pressures of sport, taking a good step in the direction of angst-free play. How? They can remind themselves that sport is not life, and life matters more. Sport *does* matter – it is big business, part of national consciousness, and inextricably bound up with the self-esteem of those who play it for a living. But it matters rather less than we imagine it does. Discovering that clichéd 'sense of perspective' remains worth the effort.

One way of doing that is to see sport as more than about the end result. Playing sport is part of personal development, your education in life. Playing sport doesn't have to be good for you, but it can be, and it's worth making it good for you if you possibly can. I am not saying that personal development is more important than winning; on the contrary, I am saying that enjoying the journey of self-discovery, by removing some of the pressure and angst associated with winning at all costs, is one way of helping you to win more often.

Trying desperately hard and not getting what you want is a decent summary of what almost all sportsmen go through. The more deeply you compete and the greater the quality of your caring (to lift a line from Philip Larkin), the more it hurts when you lose, or fail or fall short. Each time a competitor taps into the essence of his personality in an attempt to win a sports match, he takes a risk. The risk is that he will get no reward – in the sense of a win or a personal triumph – for exposing himself to that degree of psychological rawness. It is easy to resent having tried so hard in the first place.

If it didn't get us anywhere today, why should I bother to care so deeply next time? One answer is that being prepared and able to experience such deep emotions, and being exposed to that degree of disappointment, is a privilege not open to many. It doesn't feel like a privilege at the time. It feels like hell. But it makes for a life more fully lived. After ten years playing professional sport, I have come to the startling conclusion that a big part of me actually enjoys caring about sport, even when that caring expresses itself as pain at losing. I wouldn't rather life was more pallid. Stranger still, I find that knowledge reassuring, a consolation even. It sometimes reminds me that I am not wasting my time – and protects me a little from that resigned emptiness we all dread in sport.

There is a paradox here. The amateur ideal hijacked sport and co-opted it to its own means. I am advocating the opposite – taking the philosophy of amateurism and using it for the ends of professional sport.

Amateurism took many profound truths and tried to shoe-horn them into an over-arching and unified moral framework. That moral system – Corinthianism, or the amateur ideal – was strained at the best of times. Now, over a hundred years after the British began claiming sport was all about forming character and manning an empire, it is still more outdated and unconvincing.

But the contributing strands remain as true as ever. Playing with joy, without concern about the money you might earn or the criticism you may provoke, often makes sportsmen play better. An unburdened sportsman is more likely to play at his best.

Using sport as a means of self-discovery isn't the be-all and end-all of sport – it never has been and it certainly isn't in today's world. But it can help. It guards against despair and finds a silver lining in defeat – there is a new reason to dig deep and come up for more.

Focusing on the present, what you are actually doing, not the possible rewards or dangers, helps us to perform better. When we forget the burden of professionalism on our backs, as Felipe Scolari said, we rediscover that childlike freedom and instinctiveness.

Amateurism is old hat nowadays. We are all professionals – and justifying our wages requires a never-ending search for victory. But we might find a few answers, or at least better questions, in some of the more timeless and pragmatic strands of amateurism.

One point of this book is that the lessons of sport might apply to other spheres. I wonder, if you changed the word 'sport' every time it appeared in this chapter to the word 'education', whether an enlightened contemporary headteacher would think it had similar validity in the context of the new 'professional' world of teaching. And business? Or politics?

3. Zidane's kiss: why did Zizou headbutt Materazzi?

It was one of the defining images of modern sport. With eight minutes of extra time remaining in the 2006 World Cup final, the French captain, Zinédine Zidane, head-butted the Italian defender Marco Materazzi to the ground. A red card ensued, then France's defeat, followed by collective disbelief. What *was* he doing?

The timing was bizarre, to say the least. The final whistle loomed not only for the World Cup final, but also for Zidane's wondrous career. He had announced beforehand that he would retire at the end of the tournament. His virtuoso performance in the semi-final had suggested the maestro would leave the game with one last majestic imprint. Even if Zidane had drifted through the final eight minutes of extra time, he would have left football with a peerless reputation as a champion of the big occasion.

Instead, it was almost as if a great Shakespearean actor, playing King Lear at the National Theatre for the last time, interrupted his final soliloquy by punching the dead Cordelia and then announcing his life-long hatred for producers, directors and – especially – the paying public. We all like a gracious exit. However, Zidane left us scratching our heads.

So how could he – with greatness already assured and a

1998 World Cup medal already in the cabinet – do *that*? How could a 104-match veteran lose his rag just minutes before taking his last bow? What happened to the coolness that enabled him earlier in the evening to chip a penalty into the back of the net with such insouciance?

More pop psychology later – but Zizou's headbutt raised broader questions too: can a great legacy be tarnished by a single moment of madness? And in the era of the constantly rolling news story, can the paying public simply keep demanding new chapters until we finally come across an ending that we like? More centrally, does genius have a propensity to trip over into self-destruction?

In his post-headbutt interview, Zidane apologized for being a poor example to children but denied regretting his actions. We can never be sure what Materazzi said to Zidane, nor exactly what made Zidane snap, nor whether Zidane's press conference explanation was true. An informed guess is the best we can manage. But as informed guesses go, I'm not convinced by the conventional wisdom that someone as experienced as Zidane could have been provoked to end his final match in disgrace by an insult to his family. That might have been the trigger, but the deeper causes lay elsewhere.

Scratch a brilliant sportsman deeply enough and you reach a layer of self-certainty in his own destiny. The greater the sportsman, usually the more convinced he is of his own predestined greatness. The big stage means it must be his stage, victory has been prearranged on his terms, it is his destiny to win the World Cup or the Olympics or the Ashes. It might be perfectly rational for a great player to believe he has a good chance of decisively influencing the big occasion. But that isn't what he thinks. He thinks it is inevitable. After all, well-balanced self-awareness and genius seem so rarely to co-exist.

I remember watching Ian Botham play for Worcestershire in a domestic final at Lord's near the end of his career. We all imagined it would be a glorious farewell. Instead, Botham was bowled for thirty-eight by a ball that kept low. He looked in disbelief at the wicket. What was going on here? Who was responsible for this mistake? The pitch? The groundsman? Which buffoon had failed to read the preordained script correctly?

If you could bottle that self-certainty you would have the most potent winning drug. That is why champion teams so often have a talismanic force at their centre – someone who believes the match, the day and the championship have been set up in accordance with his own destiny. His self-belief radiates to the rest of the team. Zidane had exactly that quality. When France really needed something special, he believed he would do it. That belief can be so strong that not only your own team but even the opposition can fall under its spell.

It is a truism that the best players always seem to have 'more time'. One neglected explanation is that epic self-belief operates like a partial stun-gun on opponents. By the time you have finished asking, 'What the hell is he going to do now?' the champion player has stolen a head-start.

In extra time of the World Cup final, with Thierry Henry off substituted, France again looked to Zidane, almost exclusively to Zidane. We can be sure Zidane, despite being unusually exhausted and having played longer than he would in normal circumstances, shared that view. After his announcement that he would retire from international football at the end of the World Cup, the script had gone according to plan. Zidane had taken France to the final, and now France needed him to win it. One last moment of predestined brilliance was all he required.

And he almost did it. In the 104th minute, summoning up one last effort, Zidane made a decisive run into the penalty box, a cross was delivered just in time, and Zidane's soaring header sailed inevitably towards the top of the goal. Just as Steve Waugh did with his last-over century in his final Test at Sydney, Zidane had once again subordinated the day's narrative to his own. Played two World Cup finals, won two – scored twice in each final. Just as it was meant to be.

Having complied with Zidane's will thus far, the gods now finally made a mistake. The Italian goalkeeper Buffon made an inspired save in response to an inspired header. What followed was the most revealing and desperate image of the World Cup. Aimed at no one in particular, not at the keeper, not at himself, perhaps at the heavens, Zidane's face contorted into an agonized scream. It precluded the possibility of appeasement or consolation. This should not have happened, cannot have happened, must not be allowed to stand. Zidane's face resembled Edvard Munch's famous painting.

Having come this far with him, how could the gods now abandon him? But they finally went their own way, and left Zidane in solitary despair – as they eventually do everyone, even Muhammad Ali and Don Bradman.

Which would weigh more heavily on a champion's

mood – a verbal insult to his family (the kind of insult that sportsmen hear all too often and nearly always manage to ignore) or being denied, in a state of physical and mental exhaustion, what he considered to be rightfully his: the winning goal, the perfect narrative, his destiny as a two-goal double World Cup winner? The greater the inflation of a champion's willpower, the greater the deflation when it is punctured. Zidane's deflation, like his career as a whole, was on an epic scale.

It was a narrative we disliked almost as much as Zidane hated it. Of course there was a moral dimension to people's disappointment – the hero with feet of clay. But something is dearer to us even than heroes, and that is the perfect story. The audience, as if at a Hollywood preview, wanted a change of ending. So Materazzi was in the dock; lip-readers disagreed; enquiries meandered along. But though the soap opera could continue, the imprint in history was already made. Deep down Zidane knew that. So did we.

Perhaps we should also reflect on the inevitable dangers of total self-belief and conviction. Might there be a sliding scale of self-belief – with a lack of self-confidence at one end, and fully developed madness at the other? Might not great champions – or at least champions who rely on the psychological 'X' factor – usually operate just inside the acceptable far extremity of that scale? When mere mortals say something is impossible, they think 'never say die'. When most see the odds stacked against them, the special few believe that the odds count for nothing in comparison with their own strength of character. These traits we usually admire as the hallmarks of true heroes – they are the clichés of sporting hagiography.

But if one day the same sportsman trips over into full-blooded self-delusion or madness, we turn the other way, pleading moral disgust and disbelief. Muhammad Ali is a classic example. What was he doing staying in the ring for ten rounds when he was forty years old, a defenceless, declining Parkinson's sufferer, allowing himself to be beaten up by men half his age? What did he think would happen next?

The answer is, Ali didn't think, he knew. He knew that he would repeat the 'Rumble in the Jungle', when he soaked up seven rounds of punches from George Foreman that might have flattened a lesser will, then knocked out the stronger man to regain the World Championship. Ali had known he would beat Foreman, we had doubted him. He was right; we were wrong. Ali had known he would beat Trevor Berbick, we had doubted him. He was wrong, we were tragically right.

Surely his friends and advisors should have explained the situation, protected the great man from himself. Of course, but what logic could outwit a willpower like Ali's? It is not a conversation I would have relished.

It is not a long journey from total self-belief to worrying loopiness. Just as the most finely tuned elite athletes are often extremely prone to injury – like thoroughbreds without enough slack in their bodies – so too some of the greatest competitors operate only just the right side of insanity. Zidane's exit was not nearly as sad or self-destructive as Ali's. Zidane was less the victim of his own temperament, more the architect of his downfall. But the point is the same. Zidane wasn't thinking logically when he headbutted Materazzi. He wasn't thinking at all. He was acting at a level, as he often did, which was beyond the bounds of normality.

It is not just in sport that self-belief and madness are shown to be dots on the same continuum. Excessive conviction – without which there would be no gurus, no prophets, or religious founders – has a great deal in common with more conventional forms of insanity.

In *Feet of Clay: Saints, Sinners and Madmen*, the psychologist Anthony Storr explored the characteristics of charismatic guru figures. Storr used a full range of subjects. At the straightforwardly evil end of the spectrum, Storr began by analysing Jim Jones and David Koresh. Both, of course, died in awful circumstances, as they persuaded the cults they had founded to perish in collective self-destruction.

Storr then progressed to more morally ambiguous figures such as the Russian-Armenian mystic Georgei Ivanovitch Gurdjieff, and the founder of 'perceptive thinking', Rudolf Steiner. Finally, as the reader has come to see a pattern in the characters of these would-be gurus, Storr analyses Saint Ignatius of Loyola and Jesus himself.

Why do we classify some as legitimate thinkers or spiritual leaders and others as madmen? Storr summarized: 'Idiosyncratic belief systems which are shared by only a few adherents are likely to be regarded as delusional. Belief systems which may be just as irrational but which are shared by millions are called world religions.'

But if we analyse charismatic power in rational terms, evil gurus are shown to have many of the same 'positive' qualities as respected gurus. Conversely, men considered to be saints also exhibit characteristics which we usually think of as arrogant, self-deluded or fully mad.

Storr didn't wash his hands of moral judgements. But he demonstrated how the apparently mad and the apparently sane are not different in kind but simply appear in different parts of the spectrum of sanity.

What, I wonder, would Storr have made of the frighteningly self-assured racing driver Ayrton Senna? Senna took unblinking self-belief beyond the realm of conventional confidence. 'Many times,' Senna explained, 'I find myself in a comfortable position and I don't feel happy about it. I feel it is right to slow down, but something inside of me, something very strong, pushes me on, makes me try to beat . . . myself. It is . . . an enormous desire to go further and further, to travel beyond my own limits.'

Senna begins to sound like one of Storr's mystics. When he was criticized after driving a rival off the track in Japan in 1990, he simply replied, 'But I am Senna.' His mystical belief in himself was a vast part of his success. But on 1 May 1994, it was Senna's car that flew off the track. He died, tragically young at 34, perhaps still believing that nothing was beyond him.

José Mourinho, the mercurial manager of Chelsea, also takes self-belief to the borders of sanity. He is the latest top manager to place himself in the grand tradition of manager-as-mad-genius (Brian Clough mastered it first). In early 2007, he was engaged in an extended battle with the Chelsea owner, Roman Abramovich.

Put yourself in Mourinho's shoes. Your boss is a Russian billionaire who has just split from his second wife while simultaneously experiencing tensions with the unpredictable Russian president, Vladimir Putin. Your Chelsea side are having a rare dip in form. Your heralded summer signing

Andriy Shevchenko (a close friend of Abramovich) isn't having a great time of it. What do you do in these tricky circumstances?

Easy. Give an interview saying that ten of your starting eleven are 'untouchables', leaving only Shevchenko in the dispensable category. Threaten resignation unless Abramovich concedes more control. Talk to Madrid about leaving Chelsea. Generally make Putin, in comparison, seem like an avuncular voice of reason.

Perhaps Mourinho knew exactly what he was doing – and pretending to be mad is part of his magic. Alternatively, he started to believe in his own bluff to the point he forgot he was bluffing at all. It all ended, we know now, with Mourinho leaving Chelsea in September 2007.

The Times columnist Matthew Parris has also interpreted political leadership in terms of mysticism and madness:

Genius and madness are often allied, and nowhere is this truer than in political leadership. Great leaders need self-belief in unnatural measure. Simple fraudsters are rumbled early, but great leaders share with great confidence tricksters a capacity to be more than persuaded, but inhabited, by their cause. Almost inevitably, an inspirational leader spends important parts of his life certain of the uncertain, convinced of the undemonstrable . . . So do the mentally ill.

This led Parris to the subject of Tony Blair. Parris interprets Blair's capacity to convey conviction as a powerful but dubious political gift. Sorting out Africa? No problem. Solving global terrorism? I'm on the case. Better public services, no more taxes? That'll be the Third Way. By the time it is clear that Blair has not, in fact, delivered the goods, he has moved on to a fresh topic about which he can demonstrate absolute conviction. Though the subject matter keeps shifting, the self-certainty remains constant.

In 2003, as attempts to justify the Iraq war intensified, Parris argued that Tony Blair's degree of conviction without evidence bordered on insanity. 'Are we witnessing the madness of Tony Blair?' he asked.

If so, some of the guilt should lie with the audience (the electorate), not the actor (the Prime Minister). If it is true that we increasingly prefer conviction to logic or reason – he obviously truly believes it, so that counts for *something*, doesn't it? – we can have no complaints when we are rewarded with a great (if slightly unhinged) chameleon rather than a great logician.

Where conviction is concerned, it is all part of the package. How can one sports star tarnish a great career just as he leaves the stage? Why does another's irrational self-belief make him cling on far beyond the point of dignity and self-respect? We may as well ask how the poet-novelist Aleksandr Pushkin could mock the gung-ho pride of jilted lovers in his book *Eugene Onegin*, and then be shot dead in a duel himself, this time in the game of real life.

Why are we surprised when extraordinary men fail to accept the logic of an ordinary final chapter? Those who enjoy the spectacle might do well to reflect that the condition of greatness can be double-edged.

Rarely can sporting greatness have come under closer scrutiny than in the film *Zidane – A 21st Century Portrait*.

When Real Madrid played Villarreal on 23 April 2005, seventeen synchronized cameras focused exclusively on Zidane. The film, in real time, from first kick to the end, shows just Zidane's match. He never leaves our view. We are taken not only on to the pitch, but also into Zidane's imaginative world – a great player coming to the final chapter of his career.

Zidane does up his socks; he breathes heavily; he kicks his toes into the turf like Jimmy Connors used to at Wimbledon; he wipes sweat from his face; he scarcely speaks; he doesn't smile for the first hour. His only words in the first half are to the referee, immediately after the opposition have been awarded a penalty and scored. 'You should be ashamed of yourself,' Zidane says very quietly and with no emotion. In case the referee missed it, he repeats, 'You should be ashamed of yourself.'

But it is mostly everyday, unglamorous and humdrum. What, then, makes it so compelling? The answer is Zidane himself. I doubt the film would work if it featured any other footballer. But Zidane's psychological intensity carries the film.

He has a completely natural type of focus – there is no posturing, attention-seeking or affected team-spiritedness. We all know that Zidane has mastered economy of movement and clarity of thought, but here he is shown also to possess a pared-down control of emotional stimulus. 'Focus' and 'concentrate' are the two commonest sporting clichés. But rarely does anyone add that you cannot focus and concentrate on everything. The art is what you leave out.

Zidane leaves out almost everything. His detachment is

on an epic scale – that is what adds fire to his few, but decisive, moments of intervention. With Real Madrid 1–0 down, Zidane makes a mesmerizing run and sets up the perfect cross for his team-mate to head into the goal. But our view is only of Zidane – and he is expressionless as the goal is scored. It is not fake coolness. Instead, it is the genuine disinterestedness of the Zen master. He is doing his job so well, there is not space to worry about whether other people are also doing theirs.

But Zidane combines calmness with simmering street-wise aggression. There is a darkness to his concentration – he would be just fine if things got nasty, in fact he might relish it. His is not a gentle kind of Zen.

With extraordinary prescience, the film ends with Zidane playing beautiful football before becoming enveloped by red mist. He is sent off. 'Sometimes, you arrive at the stadium,' he explained, 'and you feel everything has already been decided. The script has already been written.' A year and a bit later, on a still bigger stage, again having defined the contest, the same thing would happen to him in the World Cup final.

Zidane leaves the field, and this film, with no remorse and little emotion. That seems in keeping with what we have seen. There has been something strange, almost unsettling, about Zidane's unblinking gaze throughout the film. Something is missing. Something is not quite right. There is little sign of any interest in complications or consequences – those very human preoccupations are missing. Perhaps whatever Zidane cannot master he doesn't notice.

Things are just as they are in Zidane's world. Perhaps an artificial framework of morality might obscure the truth of his athletic vision. They are two sides of the same coin. What can we make of that? How should we weigh it in the balance? But that is the language of moralists and writers, not of Zidane.

Zidane, Senna, Mourinho, Ali. Whatever we may preach about having sport in perspective and balance in all things, it is an unavoidable fact that the very best often play by different rules. But in trying to copy them, perhaps, we would find only the madness and none of the genius.

4. The curse of talent: or, what can beauty queens teach us about sport?

Don't talk to me about giftedness, inborn talents! One can name all kinds of great men who were not very gifted. They acquired greatness, became 'geniuses'

– Friedrich Nietzsche

One begins to suspect a reverse psychology ploy: parents ambitious of turning a daughter into a future Jacqueline du Pré might do well to smash up a cello in front of her

– Zadie Smith

An academic study once traced the fortunes of a generation of high-school beauty queens across America. How had the beautiful people done in the game of real life? Not very well. Fifteen years on, the high-school beauty queens were typically doing worse – in terms of wealth, careers and even happiness – than their less good-looking contemporaries. They had peaked too early. It is another version of the parable of the hare and the tortoise.

We can only speculate what went wrong. Perhaps they had found adolescence so easy that the rest of life was a slow process of disappointment. Maybe, all too familiar with childhood adulation, they crumpled at the first adult rejections. Perhaps there is something in the cliché that you can be too pretty for your own good.

How could the same principle – the curse of talent – apply to much more interesting worlds than the adult frustrations of ageing beauty queens? A baseball team, a brilliant manager and a publishing phenomenon are a good place to start. The team is the Oakland Athletics, the manager is Billy Beane and the bestseller is Michael Lewis's *Moneyball*.

Not only is *Moneyball* one of the best and most influential sports books ever written, but it also could have been subtitled, 'How being the sporting equivalent of a beauty queen ruined my career and made me turn conventional wisdom on its head.'

If you were trying genetically to construct the perfect professional sportsman, you would probably end up with someone who looked like Billy Beane. By the time he was fourteen, he was 6' 4" (six inches taller than his father), impossibly athletic and seemingly able to pick up and master any sport at will. Beane was the high-school quarterback, the star basketball player and a peerless baseball player. Michael Lewis wrote about Beane in *Moneyball*, 'He found talents in himself almost before his body was ready to exploit them: he could dunk a basketball before his hands were big enough to palm it.'

Scouts from professional baseball hovered around the schoolboy prodigy, each of them desperate to get to know Beane personally. The attention was so over-whelming that Beane would run from practice straight to a friend's house to avoid the scouts' incessant phone calls to his home.

Beane had each of the five 'tools' that baseball scouts revered: he could run, throw, field, hit, and hit with power. Beane was also intelligent, ambitious and intensely competitive. Above all, Beane had the kind of sharp features the scouts respected. Many of them still believed they could tell by the structure of a boy's face whether he would make it in professional sport. They had a phrase they used: 'the good face'. Beane had the good face.

Unsurprisingly, Beane was first-round draft pick by the New York Mets. He hoped to combine his new $125,000 salary with his admission to Stanford – but the university withdrew Beane's place once they discovered he would not be playing baseball for them. The young man's predestined greatness as a baseball player now faced no further impediments.

Except it never happened. Beane had a miserable six-year major-league career, averaging just .219 with only three home runs. He played for different teams at different levels; he tried every possible technical approach; he smashed up dressing rooms and raged against himself; he retained the aura of a superstar without the achievements. He simply couldn't hit. Michael Lewis summed up what had gone wrong for Beane: 'A wall came down between him and his talent, and he didn't know any other way to get through the wall than to try to smash a hole in it. It wasn't merely that he didn't like to fail; it was as if he didn't know how to fail.'

'Whom the gods wish to destroy,' wrote Cyril Connolly, 'they first call promising.' By 1990, Beane had had enough.

He walked from the locker room to the front office of the Oakland Athletics and became the first professional baseball player ever to pronounce the sentence: 'I quit as a player. I want to be a scout.'

The end of one of the most disappointing playing careers ushered in the beginning of one of the great managerial careers. Beane was quickly recognized as a brilliant scout and judge of players, and in 1997 graduated to far greater powers as general manager – the youngest GM in the game. The turnaround was astonishing. In 1997, the Athletics won sixty-five and lost ninety-seven games. From 2000 onward, the As consistently won around ninety games, all of this despite losing their stars every year due to having one of the smallest payrolls in baseball. In 2002, the As won 103 games – matched only by the New York Yankees, a team that cost three times as much.

How had Beane managed to mess up a playing career that 'couldn't go wrong', and then to mastermind a managerial record that was apparently impossible within the financial inequalities of major-league baseball? The answers are linked. Experiencing the first had led Beane to the solutions he used to achieve the second.

Beane's reflections on his own career had taught him to respect performance – largely because it was never demanded of him as an emerging player. Everyone assumed talent would get him through. Where he had been indulged himself, he was careful not to make the same mistake with others.

Talent, he discovered, is rated too highly. One cliché that bounced around the dressing-room walls was: 'He's got the talent, so he's bound to get better.' In fact, talent only matures when harnessed within a personality that is capable of self-improvement. And talent, ironically, has a nasty knack of protecting the talented from the urge to self-improve. Super-talented young sportsmen, never having needed resilience thus far, often lack the psychological capacity to develop it when life gets tough in the big leagues. Beane could vouch for that himself.

Conclusion one: the As stopped signing high-school prodigies who looked great in a baseball uniform and seemed predestined to 'make it', and started signing college players who had a proven track record of being able to score runs – and something going for them beyond baseball. Everyone said the As were mad. But the runs kept coming.

If talent was overrated, Beane discovered that personality was too often ignored by scouts and managers. The baseball community overestimated its own capacity to graft real psychological resilience on to inert, talented young men. But it also suffered from a reflexive fear of players who operated outside the predictable range of jock-sportsman routine behaviour. Many coaches wanted clay models to mould with their own imprints of what a champion should look like. The difficulty, of course, is that real champions want to be themselves. So while show ponies were patiently indulged by the baseball community, independent-minded performers were written off as difficult 'eccentrics'. Principle two: we'll have the eccentrics, you can keep the show ponies.

By 2002, Beane was the most sought-after general manager in baseball. He was almost hired away by the Boston Red Sox, while two of his assistants went on to become general managers themselves. In 2004, Theo

Epstein won the World Series with the Red Sox using methods devised alongside Beane at Oakland – a case of flattery by imitation. In fact, by that point almost every team was at least dabbling with what had become known as *Moneyball* methods.

Beane's personal history was central to the Oakland experiment. We never think more deeply than about our profoundest failings. They often form the foundations of our clearest analytical insights. Beane had wrestled with the reasons for his own frustrating career and come up with some original answers.

In Beane's case, the way his own career had foundered and been misinterpreted became the guiding principle of his managerial code. He concluded: the baseball system couldn't even imagine I would mess things up – but I did, despite phenomenal talent and intense ambition, so there must be fundamental flaws in the received wisdom behind the system.

If Billy Beane was the quintessential sporting beauty queen – who found adult failure unusually disorientating because he had so little previous experience of it – which successful sportsmen have been great late-bloomers?

I am tempted to say: most of them. Many of the world's greatest sportsmen learned the hard way, growing up. Michael Jordan, perhaps the greatest of them all, has often spoken about his childhood rivalry playing backyard basketball with his brother Larry. Their high-school coach summarized them in this way: 'Larry was so driven and competitive that if he had been six two instead of five seven, I'm sure Michael would have been known as Larry's brother instead of Larry always being known as Michael's brother.'

As the younger brother, Michael got used to continual defeat. When he finally did conquer his big brother, after years of coming a poor second, beating the rest of the world had been brought within reach. While at the peak of his domination of basketball, Jordan concluded, 'When you see me play, you see Larry play.'

Jordan was dropped by his high-school team. In college, he averaged only 17.7 points per game, and was passed over in the NBA draft by the Houston Rockets and the Portland Trailblazers. Then he was picked up by the Chicago Bulls, and the rest was history. When Jordan retired in 2003, he held the NBA career records for most points scored per regular-season game (31.1), points scored per playoff game (33.4), most scoring titles in a career (10), and most consecutive seasons leading the league in scoring (7).

The history of champion sportsmen is full of this younger brother syndrome. We might call it the non-beauty queen phenomenon. The former Australian captain Greg Chappell, one of the greatest and most resilient post-war cricketers, is another example. His childhood was an extended sporting battle with Ian, his older, stronger and fiercely competitive brother. Greg put his finger on it in this way:

I have no doubt that the nurture was more important than the nature in our case. Having an older brother is a mixed blessing. The lessons, particularly the coping skills, I learned in those backyard Test matches stood me in great stead many years later when confronted by one of the greatest bowling attacks ever to

have played. There is no doubt in my mind I would not
have survived through that period without the apprenticeship
I received in our backyard.

Experiencing small formative early defeats made for
subsequent lasting victories.

For others, the period of formative struggle came later.
Steve Waugh is like Greg Chappell in that he grew
up alongside a brother (Mark) who also became a great
sportsman – another backyard where the 'Tests' were pretty
fiercely fought. Waugh was certainly not made to wait too
long for advancement: he was picked for Australia at twenty
years old and earmarked as a future star.

It didn't go according to plan. Waugh encountered both
individual and team problems. The Australian eleven of
the mid- and late '80s was a struggling side which battled
on the wrong end of some pretty tough series. Waugh had
come into an Australian team that was sometimes bullied
rather than feared. He later wrote about one infamously
ill-tempered and ferocious defeat at the hands of the West
Indies: 'Our opponents' lack of humility was an image that
stuck with me. It was one I knew would motivate me at a
later date.'

Waugh has talked about the psychological consequences
of experiencing those team defeats. When it was Australia's
time to be the best in the world, partly during his captaincy,
Waugh always gave the impression that he never forgot
the blows he had taken in those early years. It is true that
Waugh inherited a great side from Mark Taylor. But he
turned the key one more notch. He made it his business
to end the days of Australia winning the series and then

losing the last Test. Winning the series wasn't enough; Waugh wanted the complete elimination of the opposition.

Individually, Waugh's career had also seen early struggles. It took a long while for him to fulfil his promise – even to the extent of being dropped in favour of his twin brother. The rest of his hugely successful career seemed to be characterized by an unflinching ruthlessness – as if he had experienced more than enough disappointment for one life already.

Formative defeats are usually a central strand in any successful sportsman's story – because failure, for almost every athlete, is written into the script. The important question is not whether you will fail, but when, and, above all, what happens next.

Billy Beane would have been intrigued by the career trajectory of a friend of mine. She started athletics quite late in childhood, and discovered an amazing natural aptitude. She got steadily better without any obvious bad spells of form. At 24 she won a Commonwealth gold medal. Soon after, she lost form and never regained it properly. Injuries, a separate career, new interests, moving on and enjoying other things in life all played a part in that. But it is also possible that she was a fully formed athlete when the first cycle of failure began. She had only known progress. Failure, when it came, was unusually disorientating. Ironically, a more chequered ascent might have prevented the irreversible pattern of her descent.

So, failure has a silver lining. Maybe the old cliché about the school of hard knocks forming character is true – as defeat can fire competitiveness, failure builds up our resilience. Perhaps it protects us from complete collapse: having watched the wheels fall off before, we should be better equipped to put them back on again. I certainly hope so.

I have known some sportsmen, having reached the same conclusion about the dangers of excessive good fortune and the long-term benefits of formative failure, to take a healthy scepticism about talent too far.

'What *is* talent? Does this talent stuff win any matches? Does it take any wickets? How many hundreds has talent got next to its name? There's only one thing more misleading than talent and that's potential.' That is what one thoughtful but argumentative senior pro used to say in the dressing room when the term 'very talented' cropped up. He wasn't untalented himself. So it wasn't jealousy.

His contempt for talent stemmed from his belief that it was a red herring. He thought too much time was wasted talking about talent. 'I don't know what talent is, but whatever it might be, it's overrated.'

His questions deserve to be answered. Here goes: talent, I think, is what you can't learn, hone or teach. Talent may be connected to skill, but it is different — a skill can be learned, talent can't. Talent is a raw mineral that is mined at birth. It is what you start with, and end up with — that which you have no control over. It is God's — or fate's — gift. To that extent, I believe in talent. I respect it. Talent can intervene at any moment in sport or the performing arts, almost without anyone's control over it. Talent is Garry Sobers; talent is Jimi Hendrix. Suddenly raw talent takes to the stage — and the measured draperies of planning and technique are excluded for a while. Talent is real all right.

But there is a core of truth beneath the old pro's exaggeration. If you took a sample of any top sports team, I think people would be surprised how few of the players had enjoyed a smooth journey to success. A professional team is almost never made up of eleven schoolboy heroes, each of whom was always earmarked as the 'one who would go all the way'.

On the way up – during the colourless trial matches, the gloomy motorway travel, the waiting to find out about being picked, the bouncing back from disappointment, the fronting up for another day of being judged and measured – the late-developers, stubborn survivors and consistent over-performers have elbowed aside quite a few of the predestined stars.

Every dressing room, of course, is made up of a complex mix of the different types. A team is a real cross-section – that is part of what makes a team interesting. Some, the winners in Darwinist selection, are so talented they were almost genetically destined to end up on the field of play. Others, who learned complementary skills precisely because they had a harder time in making it, owe their presence at the top table more to character and resilience.

Who can be surprised, occasionally, if the two types – the tortoises and the hares – look at each other and think: how on earth did we end up sharing the same world and playing the same game?

The tortoises, as the parable of the beauty queens demonstrates, often come through. So it is, too, with real kings and queens. A surprising number of effective monarchs, such as Henry VII or Henri IV of France, were older usurpers with existing experience of politics and governance. Many qualities may make a good monarch, but wariness, resilience and independence are high among them. Perhaps being worshipped from birth as the heir apparent doesn't help.

'Late promotion after years of unrequited desire,' as Mike Atherton has written about sportsmen, 'can often bring immediate reward.'

5. Does a sport have a natural home?

It is easy to think that a country ends up loving the appropriate sport, like a lock waiting for the right key. 'Cricket is an Indian game accidentally discovered by the English' is the first line of Ashis Nandy's *The Tao of Cricket*. Nandy's argument is that the religious and social context of Indian life – in particular the Hindu concept of destiny – was uniquely susceptible to cricket's laws. Cricket, Nandy argued, was all about destiny. In turn, that guaranteed cricket's destiny would have an Indian dimension.

Others have made similar claims that certain sports and countries were destined for each other. One sportswriter, beginning his report about the 2006 Ryder Cup, wrote that 'golf was an American game accidentally discovered by the Scots'. In *Beyond a Boundary*, C. L. R. James's insightful study of Caribbean cricket, there is the implication that cricket – and only cricket – was sufficiently sophisticated to fill the West Indian need for self-expression.

Cricket, of course, has also been used to explain England and Englishness, as though the two were synonymous. As Neville Cardus, with the air of one producing a rabbit from a hat, theorized:

If everything else in this nation of ours was lost but cricket – her Constitution and the laws of England – it would be possible to reconstruct from the theory and practice of cricket all the eternal Englishness which has gone to the establishment of that Constitution and the laws aforesaid.

Baseball, that most mythical of sports, has desperately cultivated an all-American image. At the Hall of Fame museum in Cooperstown, upstate New York, the first lines in the display are:

In the beginning, shortly after God created the heaven and the earth, there were stones to throw and sticks to swing. Thus, while the origins of baseball are lost to antiquity, something like it went on in prehistoric civilizations.

What is it about superpowers? Why do they insist they have invented everything? Historians in communist China were encouraged to invent historical facts to 'prove' the myth that the Chinese had invented football during the Han dynasty (206 BCE–221 CE). In truth, they invented lots of other things, but not football. The popular game *cuju*, though it contained an element of kicking a round object, was not the antecedent of modern football. Nor was it the only ancient non-European game with football-like characteristics – the Aboriginal Australians played the kicking game *Marn Gook*, the Polynesians and Micronesians kicked around balls made of Pandanus leaves, and the Native Americans played many ball games that precluded handling the ball.

How strange, then, that the President of FIFA, Sepp

Blatter, should announce at the Beijing Football Expo 2004 that 'We honour the Chinese people for their country's role as the cradle of the earliest forms of football, having firmly planted the roots of our sport and helping set the course for it to grow into the beautiful game it is today.' It went down well, unsurprisingly, in China. Should the Pacific Islanders, Native Americans and Aboriginals expect similar flattery from Mr Blatter?

Back in America, the baseball Hall of Fame, having listed a few more random postings about the history of the world with typically ponderous and plodding prose, then decrees:

Baseball, as we know it, probably had its roots in one of these early bat-and-ball games. No one knows for sure, but baseball was born in America. That we do know for sure.

Actually, we don't – more of that soon. But, more broadly, does a sport really have a natural home? Were some sports bound to flourish in certain countries, and some teams predestined to play in a particular style? It is easy to slip into ideas of inevitability after events have happened. Whether they were always going to turn out that way is another question entirely.

Take cricket and baseball. The conventional view is that nothing could be less American than cricket. And nothing could be more American than baseball. Wrong on both counts. Americans, in fact, could have ended up staying in striped caps and cricket whites. And baseball, far from being an all-American baby, may have been spawned by French monks and nuns.

Far from being an unpopular anachronism, cricket was

once America's favourite team sport. It rivalled baseball for most of the nineteenth century, with as many stories in the sports pages of the *New York Times* until 1880. Indeed, the first international cricket match was between Canada and the United States in 1844. By 1850 cricket clubs flourished in twenty-two states. And in 1858, when the architects of New York's new Central Park had to name the area allocated for ball games, they came up with 'the Cricket Ground' – much to the despair of baseball's early supporters.

What went wrong for cricket in America? Climate cannot have been an issue as summer there is perfect for cricket. Nor was North American multiculturalism a real problem. Elsewhere cricket quickly reached beyond its Englishness – Irish Australians, for example, never saw it as an Anglo-Saxon pastime.

The most common argument is that cricket was too long and slow. 'Americans do not care to dawdle – what they do, they want to do in a hurry,' argued Henry Chadwick, the Englishman who helped define baseball's early days. 'In baseball, all is lightning. Thus the reason for American antipathy to cricket can be readily understood.' But that was in 1850, when antipathy to cricket was still being invented in the American imagination.

The real answer is that baseball got a lucky bounce in the form of the Civil War. The pitch could be rougher and less equipment was needed, so bored soldiers found it easier to set up a baseball game than a cricket match. Baseball, for the first time, started to draw ahead.

Enter the spin-doctors. Baseball's most successful evangelist was A. G. Spalding, who happened to be a manufacturer of sporting goods. He marketed baseball as America's game, invented by Americans, not effete Brits. It was an honest, rugged game, not a class-ridden elitist diversion. Spalding would not be the last entrepreneur to realize that there is a big market for class-conspiracy theories. Inventing baseball's democratic heritage made him a rich man.

When his 1888 'All Star' baseball world tour returned home, they were welcomed back with a vast celebration banquet. The president of the league repeatedly announced that his sport's origins were distinctly American, unconnected with inferior English ball games. The guests began to chant: 'No rounders! No rounders!'

Spalding, wanting his populist take on baseball to be seen as revealed truth, persuaded a friendly senator to authorize him to form an investigative commission on the origins of the game. The commission announced that baseball was invented in 1839 by a Civil War hero, Abner Doubleday, in Cooperstown. A nice story, but sadly untrue. Doubleday spent the summer of 1839 as an army officer cadet at West Point, nowhere near Cooperstown.

But no one cared. America had arrived, and baseball – backed by a burgeoning sense of patriotism – had arrived with it. Cricket was guilty by association. It retreated into pockets of East Coast anglophilia, arcane strongholds of the old world order. It is a truism that the winners write history. Just as the Tudor kings demonized the 'hunchback' Richard III, baseball demonized cricket.

It is a common trend. Many sports have promoted themselves by blackening their rivals. You might imagine Gaelic football has always been so entrenched in the Irish imagination that it would have no need for such PR tricks. But in the 1870s and 1880s, 'English' sports were becoming increasingly popular – an Irish Football Union (rugby) was created in 1874, an Irish Football Association (soccer) was formed in 1880, and even cricket had eight county clubs by 1879.

How could the Irish be protected from this wave of English sports? In 1884, a group of Fenians and radical Catholic churchmen founded the Gaelic Athletic Association. People had to choose, said the GAA, between 'Irish and foreign laws'. The GAA announced that no athlete would be allowed to compete at a GAA match if he competed elsewhere under other rules.

As Archbishop Thomas Croke put it:

If we continue . . . condemning the sports that were practised by our forefathers, effacing our national features as though we were ashamed of them, and putting on England's . . . effeminate follies . . . we had better at once abjure our nationality, clap hands for joy at the sight of the Union Jack and place 'England's bloody red' exultantly above the 'green'.

The pressure and pleading worked. By the turn of the century, the GAA had a grand new stadium (Croke Park) and Gaelic football was probably the most popular game in the country. By 1914, the GAA could claim to be the single most important institution (apart from the church) in the country. How useful it is – as both baseball and Gaelic football independently discovered – to have a common enemy (those English effeminate games) to drive their cause.

Back to baseball. One remarkable possibility is its real

origins may be European and ecclesiastical. According to David Block's book *Baseball Before We Knew It*, the game may be traced to a continental ball game called *la soule*. A French manuscript from 1344 depicts monks and nuns engaged in a game that looks very like co-ed rounders. Block concludes that the field is clear for the French to claim 'parental rights over America's national game'.

I doubt they will rush to do so. But to saddle the French with inventing the game of tobacco chewing and spitting, while simultaneously debunking the myths that killed off cricket in America – what a delicious historical discovery!

Sports were not only invented in unexpected countries and flourished where you least expect; they have also taken on counter-intuitive national interpretations. Take football in Italy. Given the Italian male's susceptibility to polished Vespa mopeds, finely cut woollen suits and liberal amounts of hair product, you would expect him to play football based on display and aesthetic appeal. Italian football should, by logical extension of national stereotypes, be high on flair and low on efficiency and productivity. It should be literally 'the beautiful game'.

Instead, Italian football, for all its hair-coiffeuring and technical skill, is the most pragmatic in the world. Since the 1960s, Italy has favoured the *catenaccio* system, the lock-down. This set-up adds a sweeper as an extra layer of defence alongside the traditional back four. The sweeper is often given the specific duty of man-marking the opposition's most attacking player. The *catenaccio* starves the opposition of the ball, exhausts their creativity and finally strangles defeat from a frustrated enemy.

Gianluca Vialli, star of Italian football and once manager of Chelsea, became so fascinated by the contrasting cultures of English and Italian football that he spent two years writing a book about it. 'One of the most important aspects can be summed up in one sentence,' Vialli wrote. 'To the Italian footballer, football is a job: to the English footballer, it's a game.'

Anyone who has visited Italy will know about the expressiveness and spontaneity of its people. The English, on the other hand, are regarded as more inhibited and buttoned-up. And yet Vialli, having played in both cultures, concluded:

It's rare to see an Italian player smiling in training or on the pitch. In England, they laugh, they have fun and they still give a hundred per cent. You only need to look at the environment in the dressing room before a match. In Italy, they are tense, they are fully concentrated on the game, they are thinking about what they need to do. In England, it's like a discotheque. There is music, fun, chaos . . .

In other words, what could be less Italian than Italian football? Even when a country's footballing style does seem well suited to its population, it is often a more recent development than we imagine. At the start of the 1960s, Dutch football – far from being full of cosmopolitan sophistication – was amateurish and tactically unrefined. Ten years later, with Johan Cruyff as its figurehead, the Dutch had taken football to a new level of refinement and beauty. Cruyff played like an artist and talked in riddles. 'The game always begins afterwards,' he said, and: 'Every disadvantage has its advantages.' Everyone thought: 'How Dutch.' Who could remember the old Holland and its dull football?

Things change, and change quickly. Not long ago, Arsenal was the team of grim efficiency. 'One-nil to the Ars-e-nal', sang the North Bank. Now, after ten years under the professorial management of Arsène Wenger, they are standard-bearers of the beautiful game. Aesthetes swoon when it all clicks for Arsenal. The Gunners are the romantics of European football. Who now remembers the Arsenal of brutal pragmatism, feverish defence and the offside trap? Perhaps there are still devotees of that game, moaning into their lattes at the new Arsenal stadium. But the Arsenal fans' 'Give us back the grim old days' campaign seems a bit quiet to me. Instead, I rather suspect they loved Thierry Henry's dazzling runs and Arsenal's new cosmopolitan swagger.

Clubs change their spots; so too countries change their tastes – about sport as about everything else. The most entrenched style can quickly reinvent itself. In communist Ukraine, their national coach, Valeri Lobanovsky, developed a system of play where every action was given a definite 'value'. Pass – tick. Tackle – tick. Corner – tick. Chase – tick. It was football by Marxist rationality. The real value of these 'values' didn't come into the equation. A pass back was worth as much as a pass forward, or a goal-making assist.

Players sought to gather 'points' rather than goals, and the easiest way to do that was in a high-energy defensive game. Lots of organized rushing around – that was the way to earn 'points'. Putting your foot on the ball and looking for the decisive opening? Where was the value in that?

Then, in the aftermath of communism's collapse, Ukrainian football embraced something approaching a free transfer market. Which players did the teams rush to sign? Hard-working English terriers? No, Nigerian playmakers – who play the most unstructured and intuitive game in the world. By 2001, nine Nigerians were signed to play in the Ukrainian premier league. Ukrainian football would never be the same again.

Football, in fact, has proved particularly adept at reversing common stereotypes. In the 1970s and '80s, as more black players had success with English clubs, football's racists needed a way to explain white supremacy while still tolerating the idea that their team's black players served a purpose. They settled on the more subtly racist idea that black players might be skilful going forward, but didn't have the 'character' to play well in defence. That racist fantasy didn't hold up, either. The right back Viv Anderson, when he played against Czechoslovakia at Wembley in 1978, became the first black man to play for England. By 2006/7, teams like Arsenal often played an all-black back four.

Sport consistently confounds rather than reinforces national and racial stereotypes. Sports frequently flourish where you would least expect; and they often change their geographical axis of power, just as countries reinvent the brand of sport they play. Few predicted soccer would take off in Africa, or that cricket's powerbase would shift to the Indian subcontinent, or that baseball's major leagues would have Japanese players. It is an unpredictable, fluid process of evolution – hard to explain, even harder to predict.

★

Games are more interchangeable than we like to think. Indulging cricket's democratic myths, the historian G. M. Trevelyan argued that 'If the French noblesse had been capable of playing cricket with their peasants, their chateaux never would have been burnt.' Trevelyan may have been half right, but not in thinking that cricket possesses peculiar anti-revolutionary balm or the power to promote reasonable debate. Perhaps a game of pétanque might have done the job just as well.

John Major, a serious cricket fan, in fact so serious that he has three red cricket balls on his coat of arms, has argued that 'Fifty years from now, Britain will still be the country of long shadows on county grounds, warm beer, invincible green suburbs, dog lovers and pool fillers, and – as George Orwell said – "old maids cycling to Holy Communion through the morning mist".'

Thirteen years on – his hypothesis has thirty-seven left to run – it may be doubtful whether Major's vision of Britain will survive. But national traits rarely do. In medieval times, foreign chroniclers bemoaned the English, even the English court, as unrefined, coarse and unschooled in proper manners. And yet when England became the pre-eminent nation of empire, it was synonymous – however hypocritically – with gentlemanliness, deference, and a code of behaviour.

Stereotypes not only evolve – they also reverse. So it is with sports. There will come a time when a golfer is caught deliberately cheating, and justifies his actions by saying it is a professional world and you must do what you can get away with – his mistake was not cheating, he will say, but getting caught. There will be much hand-wringing up on golf's moral high ground, but it will happen. A sport's culture is always evolving, always subject to new interpretation – often for the good, sometimes for the bad.

Games are also more amorphous than we care to admit, even in our private thoughts. We like the idea that a game's culture is built from stern stuff – impregnable against invasion or decay. It is reassuring to feel that a game's identity, especially an identity we like, is ring-fenced and secure.

But it is wrong. Lord Harris thought that 'cricket was more free from anything sordid, anything dishonourable, than any game in the world.' The same game, a century or so later, faced widespread investigations into match-fixing and bribery.

A truer and wiser view was put to me by a former Australian cricketer. 'I have played, followed and loved cricket all my life,' he said to me. 'But there are times when I wonder what I would feel if cricket receded in the popular imagination, and was overtaken by – say – baseball or something else. I would be sad personally, but not for proper logical or intellectual reasons. And I would get over it. So long, that is – and it is a big if – that the new sport had a culture worth supporting and that it was a game I would want my grandchildren to play. It is the culture that matters.'

It was one of the most poignant things I had heard about sport. As with many pragmatic views, within the realism, there are reasons for hope and grounds for action. If we like a game how it is, or how it has become, we must make sure we preserve what is good even as we accept the inevitability of change. Nothing stands still, especially in sport. Flux is constant, and every sport's identity, even as I write, is being fought over and defined.

Cultures, sporting and otherwise, are always in the balance. 'If you want things to stay as they are,' as di Lampedusa writes in *The Leopard*, 'things will have to change.'

6. Why history matters in sport (and how England won the 2005 Ashes)

It seems strange, in the aftermath of the reversal that was to follow, to write about the great Ashes victory of 2005. But those who doubt what cricket means to the English should have been at the Oval on 12 September 2005, or in London that evening or the following day, or almost anywhere in the country during the whole summer. The Ashes was not only the greatest series of our age. It also captured the English imagination in the strange and myriad ways that only cricket can.

The subsequent 5–0 Ashes defeat of 2006/7 in Australia was so disappointing that it prompted an independent inquiry. Perhaps that should have come after 2005. It may not always be true that we learn from defeat rather than victory. The most revealing stories tend to be surprises, shifts in an accepted trend. If you lose nine out of ten series, it is the one, not the nine, which would most interest a historian.

So whose triumph was it? The players', the coaches' or the administrators' – perhaps even the people's? Of the many factors which led to England's epic victory, which were the most important? Was it destiny, strategy, leadership or a little bit of luck? How did England win the Ashes in 2005?

According to the former England skipper Nasser Hussain it was down to the coach, Duncan Fletcher. Chris Adams, captain of Sussex, felt England's resurgence owed much to the improved standard of county cricket. To students of physics and mechanics, the answer lay in the mysterious business of reverse swing. To arch-sceptics, it was pure luck: Australia were in a dominant position in the Ashes until Glenn McGrath suffered a freak ankle injury just before the start of the second Test. More generous spirits believed in the power of leadership – the Ashes belonged to Michael Vaughan. To the many men on the street, it was simpler still: England had a true hero again, a man called Andrew Flintoff.

Suppose a group of great historians addressed the issue, what would they conclude? We could expect a lively argument, of course – because historians never agree. And in arguing about the Ashes, our historians would reveal their own historical perspectives and intellectual prejudices. We could then use the Ashes as a hypothetical case study into history itself: how can the same events provoke such different – and often contradictory – explanations? In other words, what can history teach us about sport, and what can sport teach us about history?

A Whig historian, perhaps a latter-day Macaulay or Gibbon, would look for a great over-arching theory to explain England's Ashes triumph. His findings would be published as a six-volume masterwork entitled *The Decline, Fall and Re-Emergence of the British Sporting Empire*. This historian would have a liking for long-term theories and the big sweep (the big sweep of time, that is, not Kevin Pietersen's big slog sweeps for six). He would believe that progress – and hence winning – derived from a burgeoning meritocracy in modern English sport. British sport, the Whig would suggest, had previously suffered a relative decline due to the emergence of New World sporting powers. While England had languished in a collective hangover from the class-ridden days of the professional–amateur divide, countries like Australia had moved past us. They did not have a residue of class-ridden associations at the core of their sports.

Only in the run-up to the 2005 Ashes, the Whig would conclude, had England caught up in terms of broadening the sporting franchise – and were now reaping the rewards of victory. Just as parliamentary democracy brought peace and prosperity in the nineteenth century, the Whig would say that eliminating class-ridden anachronisms is bringing sporting success in the twenty-first. (His next book is called *Changing the Dress Code at the LTA*, subtitled *How England Can Produce a Home-Grown Wimbledon Winner*.)

To a rival academic, this time an institutional or administrative historian, the Ashes triumph would have been all about the recent restructuring of the English game. His book would be called *Reform and Reformation: English Cricket 1997–2005*. For this administrative historian, the key would be found in elite institutions: systems, not men, would be decisive. Reforming English cricket's top tier would be the subject of his study.

This administrative historian would look to praise the architects of institutional reform. *Raising the Standard*, Lord MacLaurin's 1997 proposed restructuring, made an early contribution to the climate of change. There would also be a chapter on Mike Atherton's suggestion (as early as the winter of 1995/6) that there should be central England contracts. Changing the county championship – two divisions with promotion and relegation – would be another stepping stone to enlightened reform. And the new National Academy, started by Rod Marsh as a breeding ground for Test players, would receive detailed treatment.

There would be one final eulogy, this time for the money men. Even the best institutions, our administrative historian would conclude, need plenty of money. Just as Henry VIII's Thomas Cromwell needed the cash from the dissolution of the monasteries to re-brand the Tudor monarchy, so the ECB needed Sky and Channel 4. The last chapter of *Reform and Reformation* would be called 'Money Talks'.

The nineteenth-century historian Thomas Carlyle would have thought the opposite. He would have had no interest in the institutional backdrop or invisible power-brokers. Great men would have been his subject – the charismatic heroes and talismans of England's victory. He would have delighted in the iconic role of Andrew Flintoff, the confidence of Kevin Pietersen, and the authority of Michael Vaughan. 'The history of the world,' argued Carlyle, 'is but the biography of great men.' Carlyle certainly would not have minded the odd indiscretion or controversy. He believed the heroism of great men derived from their creative force, not their moral perfection. Carlyle might even have interpreted the England team's epic partying after the Ashes victory as further evidence of their great creative energy. Carlyle would certainly be clear on one point: the men on the pitch won the Ashes, no one else.

A counter-factual historian would take the opposite line. He would unpick your presumptions with carefully considered *what ifs*. What if Glenn McGrath *hadn't* twisted his ankle on a misplaced cricket ball before the Edgbaston Test? What if Ricky Ponting, having won the toss, *hadn't* decided to bowl first? By the time the counter-factual historian had finished, you might be uncertain if England really *had* won the Ashes after all. Was it really Michael Vaughan who raised the Ashes urn at the Oval? Perhaps it was Ricky Ponting?

More importantly, you would also probably have lost faith in the over-arching theories of the Whigs, administrative historians and Carlylians. History, the counter-factual thinker would have demonstrated, is more complicated and surprising than big one-size-fits-all theories allow for. It all could have been very different but for crucial interventions by chance, luck and contingency. The counter-factual history book would be called *What If Glenn McGrath Had Looked Where He Was Walking?* There would be a subsequent editorial on the comment pages of the *Sunday Telegraph* and a spin-off reality TV show called *Cleopatra's Nose and Glenn McGrath's Ankle: A Game of Chance and Adventure*.

There are two serious points here. First, people don't agree about the past. They do not agree about the weighting of causes, the decisive moment, or even the intellectual framework of the debate. Most arguments in sport and in history are not about what happened but about what matters.

Secondly, why should we care about reasons and explanations? Isn't winning enough in itself? Given that we did win the Ashes in 2005 – and the cricket was so thrilling – why bother to analyse it?

But if you were to ask why England *failed* to win the Ashes from 1987 to 2005 – and again in 2006/7 – most fans and cricket writers would agree that was a question worthy of serious consideration. And yet it is exactly the same question as why England *did* win in 2005 – only in reverse form. Instead of asking why the war has started, we have instead questioned why the peace failed. The substance of the debate is identical: professionalism in English sport, the county structure, needing star players, the role of luck and chance.

If England suffered from the absence of a galvanizing hero in the '90s, then Flintoff's emergence must have serious significance; if the combination of Warne and McGrath in tandem has usually made the difference for Australia, then McGrath suffering a freak injury is a pretty large slice of luck for the opposition. Why we didn't win the Ashes; why we did win the Ashes: the two questions can only be considered in tandem.

Throughout the latter stages of those nineteen barren years without an Ashes series win, speculating on the 'decline' of English cricket was a bar-room cliché. Everyone had an opinion, usually lots of opinions. These ranged from believing that no longer playing on uncovered wickets was ruining English batting techniques, to the conviction that smiling during cricket matches was indicative of inner meekness.

If we are ever going to win the Ashes, the pub bore began, we have to have (delete according to prejudice):

'more mental toughness/uncovered wickets/no county cricket/an Australian mentality/a new Ian Botham/blah blah blah . . .'

Pub bores can move on to the next moan without pausing for reflection. But the job of the historian is to reach beyond the level of cliché. 'So we did win the Ashes,' he asks; 'how did we do it – and how might we do it more often?' If you don't think that matters, then you probably won't be reading this anyway.

And yet there is a natural scepticism about history within the sporting world. Many people instinctively agree with Henry Ford's dictum that 'history is bunk'. Dressing rooms abound with forward-looking sayings: we live to fight another day; keep looking onwards and upwards; best not to dwell too much; after all, yesterday has gone now and there's nothing we can do about it.

A forward-looking mentality is usually regarded as the perfect sporting temperament. Conversely, thinking too much about the past has fatal associations with the forbidden sins of nostalgia, self-indulgence and introspection. We can certainly understand why sportsmen, like actors and all other types of performers, look forward wherever they can.

But though the only triumphs we can control lie in the future, the answers may not. The past is a treasure trove of information waiting to be ordered analytically into judgements. If we are to have the best chance of doing well in the next match or championship, it can only help to have a proper understanding of what went well and badly in the previous ones. Good judgement about the past – though it cannot perfectly predict the future or guarantee success – may help us to get the right strategy for the challenges ahead.

By the same logic, bad history means bad analysis of the past, and bad analysis of the past makes for poor strategy. Poor strategy costs games. History matters.

Bad history in sport takes four classic forms: simple forgetfulness; using the wrong facts and missing the real ones; using the right facts but interpreting them wrongly; the fallacy that what happened was always inevitable.

Simply forgetting

Forgetfulness is the most obvious. We all suffer from it. Professional sport is a relentless cycle of journeys, practice sessions, team-talks and matches. Motorways merge in the mind. Hotel foyers blur in the memory. Bags are constantly packed, unpacked, left behind. Forms are signed, bills paid. The road is as much home as home itself. Flux disorientates; pressure numbs; memories fray. Who can be surprised if instant and accurate recall of distant events is not always a sportsman's defining characteristic?

But too much forgetfulness borders on neglect. In a quiet moment at practice, I once got chatting with a friend and colleague about his bowling. He wondered if I had any view on why he had bowled significantly better in some phases of his career than others. Could I see a pattern or a cause?

As I knew him well and saw his form as central to our chances as a side, I quite easily reeled off the details of his last four seasons – very good, good, okay, good. I mentioned a few spells of form within the good years – I didn't analyse them, I merely remembered them. Laughing, he interrupted me: 'You know, I wouldn't have been able to remember any of those phases. I've played so many games that many of them have lost their individual identity.' As he is highly intelligent and analytical, I was amazed. How could you even start to analyse causes of good form until you could remember *when* you were in good form in the first place?

A few years on, having played many more games myself, I can see how the past becomes more blurred when there is so much more of it to blur. I also understand better that the past shouldn't be a burden. But I'm still sure that in terms of team strategy and individual self-improvement, history is an underused resource.

Knowing half the facts, and missing the important ones

A batsman is in bad form and scoring few runs. He is eaten up with anxiety and nerves. Terrified of getting out, he sets himself to defend every ball and never attack. This means he gets himself into contorted positions as he plays his shots. With each mistimed shot, he is more determined not to 'give it away'. As a result, he is so late in getting into attacking positions that every time he takes on a positive shot it seems to get him out.

One day, a colleague finally loses his temper with the player – stop giving it away, he says, show some real resolve, value your wicket, get stuck in, show some character, be a gritty professional, tough it out . . .

But the same day, a different team-mate asks the struggling batsman how he is doing. It is the first time anyone has actually asked him what he is going through in his bad patch of form. The struggling batter articulates what he has been bottling up – how he is over-anxious to do well, putting too much emphasis on success, struggling to relax at the crease, missing out on shots that he has always played well, and not even enjoying the game.

The team-mate listens and doesn't say much. When he does reply, he merely says that he has been through exactly the same feelings himself. He doesn't have any specific technical solutions. Instead, he reminds him that cricket is a game of instinct, that the easiest way to play is in the manner that he has played best throughout his career. Play like *you* play, he says, not like other people want you to play.

The next day, the struggling batter returns to form and bats like his old self – he doesn't play recklessly, but the shots he does play he is relaxed and positive enough to execute well. He gets runs, and the cycle of bad form is broken.

The colleague who shouted at him now reckons he's made the difference and feels pretty pleased with himself. (He is 100 per cent wrong, but never mind.) Well done, mate, he says. Lucky I had a bit of a go at you yesterday – it obviously got the best out of you . . .

I am not saying that the softly-softly, good-cop approach always succeeds. But I am mocking the idea that people know all the reasons behind what converts failure into success. If things do turn around, look for the link between cause and effect, not merely what happened beforehand.

In the case of the struggling batter, far more important than any technical changes – let alone any extra 'determination' that he was told to demonstrate – might have been his relaxed demeanour at the crease, or the fact that he seemed calm and happy in the dressing room. The *symptom* might have been better shot-selection and better shot-execution, but the *cause* was a more positive and relaxed mindset, a less anxious approach, a refreshed spirit, and an unburdened mind.

Chronology is not causality. Lots of things happen in the lead-up to games. Only a very few of them make any difference at all. Above all, we should be cautious when we claim a special knowledge of cause and effect. Be pretty sceptical about your capacity to be sure why things change.

Post hoc, ergo propter hoc – 'after this, therefore because of this' – that is the fallacy to avoid. And, no, I'm not a classical scholar, but Jed Bartlett said it on *The West Wing*.

Using the right facts, but interpreting them wrongly

One of the fascinations of sport is that intelligent people can look at the same game and see completely different things. This is particularly true of one of sport's most sophisticated arts: batting technique in cricket. We can all agree (usually) about *whether* someone is playing well or badly. The disagreements start when it comes to *what* is making someone play well or badly.

It's because his head is still; it's because he is keeping

side-on; it's because he is well balanced; it's because he is moving his feet more; it's because he's trusting himself and not moving his feet too much. When we see good technique, and seek to analyse it, we place our favourite batting theories at the core of the explanation.

Sometimes we can all be partially right. But, in other instances, TV evidence takes the argument into the realm of objective knowledge. Some theories are truer than others.

One of the most interesting parts of Duncan Fletcher's book *Ashes Regained* concerned Michael Vaughan's batting technique. Vaughan was not scoring many runs at the start of the 2005 season, and many pundits were trying to explain why. The commonest explanation was that he was moving too much and standing insufficiently still before the ball was bowled. One commentator, Barry Richards – a truly great batsman and an intelligent analyst – put it clearly: 'Michael Vaughan should go back to what he was doing in Australia a couple of winters ago – standing still before the ball was bowled.'

In his book, Fletcher, who works closely with Vaughan, explains that wasn't true. In Australia in 2002/3, when Vaughan's batting may have been as good as any Englishman's over the past couple of decades, he was doing the same preliminary foot movements before the ball was bowled. But he was doing them at the right time, in rhythm with the arrival of the ball. In fact, his rhythm and preliminary movements were so good that they created the *illusion* of stillness.

In that respect, Richards was right. Vaughan at his best appeared to be still. Great players are good at achieving that illusion. When people say great batters have 'more time' they are hinting at the illusion of stillness. It is a stillness achieved by not needing to move in a rushed way at the last minute. How is that stillness achieved? Often, it is caused by moving earlier. In other words, to achieve stillness it is necessary to move. Counter-intuitive, but true.

So what are the solutions? First, don't think about feet. They don't hit the ball. Saying to yourself, 'Move your feet', as the bowler is running up doesn't work, even in practice. But saying, 'Be ready' – which is meant to make sure you don't do the preliminary movement too late – is a better idea.

Stillness and balance, though they are central to good batting, are rarely achieved either by trying to 'stand still' or 'move your feet'. Good balance and good foot move-ment are the results – *symptoms* again – of batters who have good rhythm. Rhythm, as we have seen, is often associated with preliminary movement and, above all, a positive mindset. A positive mindset leads batters to take up the good body positions that are crucial to good defensive play as well as good attacking play.

That's why, for most of us, the best thing of all to say to yourself as the bowler is running up is 'Watch the ball' – because it is only by watching the ball that we can hit it in the middle of the bat.

So when people say to me, 'You're not still enough,' or 'You're not moving your feet enough,' I want to reply, 'You're looking at the symptoms – how about the causes?' Instead, tell me to go into the nets and find some rhythm by making sure I am: 1) ready by the time the ball is bowled; 2) looking to be positive and hit the ball in the middle of the bat; 3) watching the ball and not worrying about my feet.

Why can't I just say that to myself? I try to.

The fallacy of inevitability

The final type of bad history is the fallacy of inevitability. People happily throw around explanations of events without even the pretence of linking cause and effect. 'We were destined to win this year after training so hard at pre-season' is a common type of non-sequitur. What if there were pre-seasons when we trained equally hard and didn't win anything? A hard-working pre-season, in other words, might have been part of the explanation of winning – but it obviously wasn't the decisively causal reason because other equally good pre-seasons didn't bring victory. Conclusion: time to look elsewhere for explanations of success.

In the same way, after a thrilling last-ball victory, comments like 'We were *always* winning that one' often pass as revealed truth. Were we? Even if we did play with great belief, it might still be bad history: the truth about why things happen is usually much more unpredictable than that.

As Johan Huizinga put it: 'The historian must . . . constantly put himself at a point in the past at which the known factors will seem to permit different outcomes. If he speaks of Salamis, then it must be as if the Persians might still win; if he speaks of the coup d'état of Brumaire, then it must remain to be seen if Bonaparte will be ignominiously repulsed.'

The starting point of counter-factual history is what if things *hadn't* worked out as they did. A good counter-factual argument demonstrates that events could have turned out very differently, and nearly *did* take the other course.

What ifs, so often written off as mere intellectual game-playing, are in fact sometimes the perfect way to discover which causes were central and which merely incidental. What you consider to be decisively causal determines what you focus on; what you focus on decides what you do; what you do affects whether you win. Understanding causes helps to win more matches. In sport, as in all organized pursuits of excellence, history matters.

I'll end with one particularly strange counter-factual. It is unusual because people tend to use counter-factuals to exculpate themselves from blame and show how luck was against them. (What if Ed Smith hadn't been unluckily given out in that Test match at the Oval?) Instead, this *what if* draws attention to the fault of the person making the argument – but for a very good reason.

It is the argument about Shane Warne that if he *hadn't* dropped Kevin Pietersen on 15 at the Oval, Australia would have retained the Ashes. Pietersen, of course, went on to make 158 and put England into an impregnable position.

I doubt Warne even *minds* the idea his dropped catch may have turned a drawn series into a 2–1 defeat. Why? First, because Warne can be certain – dropping Pietersen notwithstanding – what a massive positive force for Australia he had been throughout the series. Secondly, he got his own back soon enough in 2006/7, and appropriately retired with his hands on the Ashes urn. Thirdly, by highlighting how the series may have hinged on one incident, deep into the story's final chapter, Warne could challenge the broader explanations that many people believe led to England's victory. Don't get too fancy with your grand theories about English resurgence, Warne might argue. (Another counter-factual historian, perhaps?)

So when we argue about history in sport, we argue about what matters. By thinking about what matters, we improve our grasp of what happened, how it happened, and how that knowledge can influence the challenges that lie ahead.

I am certainly not arguing that history – within sport, or anywhere else – can perfectly predict the future. That is because neither history nor sport is an exact or 'natural' science. They both involve human beings, and human beings – unlike particles in an experiment – are unique and often behave against type.

But history is about more than simple crystal-ball gazing. It is not just a means of identifying past 'causes' of defeat or victory, but also a way of training our critical senses to identify how new causes, or new configurations of factors, will operate now or in the future. The uses of history, in other words, go far beyond invoking past strategies and extend to imagining future ones more creatively. 'Staying ahead of the game', quite literally.

7. Is the free market ruining sport?

'The financial results of the past season prove that salaries must come down. We believe that players insisting on exorbitant prices are injuring their own interests by forcing out of existence clubs which cannot be run and pay large salaries except at a personal loss.'

No, that is not a joint statement by Roman Abramovich – having had second thoughts about the amount of money he spends on Chelsea – and the chairman of ailing Watford. In fact, it was issued on 19 September 1879 by the National Baseball League. Well over a century ago, owners of sports teams were getting stroppy about players being paid too much.

More importantly, the owners justified their point with the principles of competitive balance. A one-sided league, where the best players gravitated to the highest bidders, made for one-sided matches. One-sided contests were bad for business, bad for clubs and bad for players. The free market, they were arguing, is bad for competitive balance and bad for sport.

In truth, the free market certainly wasn't bad for players, and – before readers begin writing to the sports clubs they support demanding people like me have their wages axed – we shall see it isn't necessarily bad for sport.

But the owners won round one. In 1880, to remedy the 'evil' of higher salaries, they agreed a 'reserve clause' to stop players moving clubs. Under the reserve-clause agreement, if a player declined the terms of the contract he was offered, then no other team would be able to sign him. In other words, a baseball player signed to a team for life. You played for your existing club until they 'traded' you or sacked you, or you didn't play baseball at all. Bargaining with the club by bringing other offers to the negotiating table was out of the question – so too was simply making a fresh start at a new club.

The clause caused periodic spats between players and their clubs. But conflict reached new heights in 1969 when Curt Flood, a prolific player and co-captain of the St Louis Cardinals, was traded to the woeful Philadelphia Phillies. Flood was outraged at this cursory treatment and refused to play for his new team. The Cardinals dug in and invoked the 'reserve clause'.

'I do not feel I am a piece of property,' Flood wrote to the Commissioner of Baseball, 'to be bought and sold irrespective of my wishes. I believe any system that produces that result violates my basic rights as a citizen.'

Flood, a black man from Houston, Texas, intended his use of the term 'property' to be incendiary, and throughout the case, which ended up in the Supreme Court, he likened the reserve clause to slavery. Though Flood eventually lost the Supreme Court case 5–3 (one justice stood down), the reserve clause was fatally weakened. Flood's personal playing career was effectively ruined, but he had paved the way for the era of free agency.

When the end of the reserve clause finally came in 1975,

baseball players, and by default athletes in other sports, were about to become richer than they had ever imagined. In 1969, the minimum salary for a major-league player was $7,000. Now, star players like Derek Jeter and Albert Belle earn in excess of $10 million each year. The average salary is over $2.5 million. Effectively, the players now receive a large share of the revenue they generate.

The governing boards of English sports had also resisted the free flow of player mobility. County cricket, for example, though it turned fully professional in the 1960s, found ways to prevent players from moving clubs. Even when I started in 1996, there was a system called List I and List II. Though players were supposedly free to move counties, the county clubs had an agreement where they would only sign two List I players in any given five-year period. It was a moderate and compromised version of the reserve clause.

Not surprisingly, counties were keen to put their own top players, who might want to leave, on to List I. This had the effect of diminishing their chances of getting a deal elsewhere – not through any fault in their play but simply because any List I signing was a buyer's gamble. Given that so few List I signings were permitted, there was huge pressure on the purchasing clubs to get them absolutely right. As a result, many transfers never materialized.

There was an obvious upside to low player mobility in that counties retained more of their home-grown players, and the link between the county's community and its sports team remained strong. In fact, many felt that was one of county cricket's great strengths. But the List system stopped coaches from assembling the teams they wanted, and made it hard for top players to find a new challenge when they were at the peak of their careers. More critically, it bordered on restraint of trade and could never survive today's labour laws.

Just like the Bosman ruling of 1995 that revolutionized soccer transfers, the List system was abolished in 2003. Cricket, like soccer and baseball, then had had its own mini-version of wage escalation. The numbers are minuscule in comparison, but the principle − the removal of market protectionism leading to increased player mobility and higher salaries − is the same.

Cricket's new free market has also challenged some received opinions. Batsmen, for example, have historically enjoyed a privileged glamour within cricket. Indian princes, though they briefly tried their hand at fast bowling, quickly settled on batting as the correct order of things. When *Wisden* named its five greatest cricketers of the twentieth century − Bradman, Hobbs, Sobers, Richards and Warne − three were batsmen, one an all-rounder and only one first and foremost a bowler. Even Warne, recognizing how low his art form had sunk in the popular imagination, has said that making spin bowling cool again has been one of the most satisfying achievements of his career.

But though fans and adulation might gravitate to batsmen, the market suggests bowlers are rated more highly. Since increased player mobility started to come into cricket in the '90s, the trend has been towards greater rewards for bowlers. A proven bowler, even one who has struggled for some form or fitness, can nearly always find himself a decent county contract − in fact, they are often fought over by rival bidders. Batsmen, on the other hand, apart from occasional stand-out performers, are regarded as easier to pick up as bargains. According to the market, it is bowlers who are most valuable.

In the case of American football, the emergence of freer labour markets led to astonishing shifts in received opinion. Effectively, the market led to a reassessment of how football matches are won. Sports, like trading markets, occasionally throw up inefficient 'blind spots' – areas where conventional wisdom underestimates the true value of one piece of the strategic jigsaw.

These neglected corners of the game, like undervalued stock, provide a systematic opportunity. Every coach tries to have better tactics than his opponent. But if you're playing a superior *system* – a more efficient form of the game – then mere tactics appear like small fry. One way to win, in other words, is to find that inefficient blind spot, buy in the talent on the cheap, stick with your strategy – and count the wins and the plaudits.

This thinking-investor method of victory has attracted the close attention of the former Wall Street trader turned sportswriter Michael Lewis. For Lewis, the evolution of sport and its dramatic clashes of ideas are closely linked to the influence of the market.

In *The Blind Side*, Lewis examines how Bill Walsh, all-conquering former coach of the San Francisco 49ers, realized that everyone was looking at the wrong end of the field. The crowd, and the football community, naturally watched the glamour players – the quarterback and the wide receiver, the latter whose job it was to complete the eye-catching passes that are the visual highlight of football matches.

The quarterback, like rugby's fly half, is the most glamorous position of all. He is the decision-maker, the focal point and the conductor of the attacking ('offensive') team. The moments that win football matches often involve decisive interventions by a quarterback, so they have always been regarded as match-winners. Unsurprisingly, quarterbacks have always been among the highest-paid players.

But throughout football history, the men on whom the quarterback depends for protection – his offensive linemen, in particular the left tackle – were scarcely evaluated individually at all. They were just those huge guys who scrabbled around in the mud making sure the superhero quarterback that they protected didn't get hurt. The lot of the offensive lineman since the creation of football, as Michael Lewis wrote in his book about strategic evolution in football, was 'to be cast as the unassuming, union card-holding, lunch pail-toting blue-collar worker'.

Walsh's insight was that the quarterback might have thrown the ball, but it was his offensive linemen – effectively the quarterback's private guards – who enabled him to do so. Post-Walsh, coaches increasingly understood that without good offensive linemen, the quarterback doesn't get much of a chance to throw the ball anyway because he's face down in the mud being mauled by three wildly aggressive opponents. Proof: the San Francisco 49ers won just as many games in 1987 with their reserve quarterback. Conclusion: buy better offensive linemen.

As salaries exploded in the NFL, no one was surprised that quarterbacks became even more wildly expensive. What no one predicted was the trickledown effect on the pay of left tackles. In fact, it made perfect market sense. The price of protecting quarterbacks, as Lewis concluded, 'was driven by the same forces that drove the price of other kinds of insurance: it rose with the value of the asset insured, with the risk posed to that asset'.

So in the 2006 Super Bowl, the highest-paid player, inevitably, was the Seattle quarterback, but the *second* highest-paid player was the left tackle who protected his blindside – Walter Jones. (It is the quarterback's blindside which is most vulnerable to being hit by opposition players.) Many fans didn't know anything about Walter Jones (or any other left tackles), or had much idea what he was doing out there. Jones had no celebrity endorsements or star status. Very few people, being naturally preoccupied with the players who handle the ball, even bothered to watch what Jones was up to. But to the minds trying to win the Super Bowl, the coaches and general managers who were writing the cheques, the left tackle was the second most valued player on the pitch – a radically different answer from any that would emerge from a fans' poll.

So the free market has a far more subtle influence on sport than simply giving athletes more money. It has also discovered some sportsmen are more essential than received wisdom previously imagined, and others more replaceable. The market, once unleashed, cannot be restrained from challenging accepted opinion – what the economist Joseph Schumpeter called the 'waves of creative destruction'. 'Football common sense', the old wisdom of most fans and football insiders, had been quite wrong.

It is often wrongly assumed that the free market is always on the side of life's heavy hitters. But sport gives plenty of examples that it is the market which corrects received wisdom in favour of untrumpeted stars. The internet has done something similar in publishing. Amazon.com has limited the power of publishing houses to 'decide' which of their books will succeed (we authors yearn for that big advertising budget that gives the all-important initial push) by allowing minority books which are actually read (not just bought and discarded) to survive long after old-fashioned bookstores would have been able to keep stocking them. The broader, internet-based market has opened up publishing to a more genuinely democratic market than it had ever known before.

Lewis explored a connected theme in his widely influential book *Moneyball* about how the market was made to re-evaluate how baseball matches are won. Enjoying the conceptual framework of *Moneyball*, fortunately, requires no understanding of baseball itself. The story reached out far beyond the confines of American sport. Even the *Spectator* – scarcely a dedicated baseball magazine – ran two longish reviews. *Moneyball* had become a metaphor for independent thinking, the scientific method and especially the free market. What influence could these ideas have on the cobwebbed superstitions and inefficiencies of an unreformed community?

Baseball, it should be explained at the outset, is not a fair game. Money helps. The New York Yankees – the game's aristocrats – have a payroll three times bigger than that of the impoverished Oakland As. The Yankees simply buy the best players. The As had to come up with a different way to win. They had to find the flawed champions that the sporting village underestimated and hence under-priced. As we saw in chapter 4, the As needed to find a scientific strategy for picking up bargain athletes on the free market.

The As also re-examined how a game is won. Received wisdom – such as the truism that games are won by pitchers not batters – proved not to be so wise after all. They demonstrated how often baseball 'wisdom' bordered on superstition.

Baseball, for those who don't know, is perhaps the only sport in which statistics are followed even more obsessively than in cricket. Forget poring over the pages of *Wisden*: baseball fans bring a whole new complexion to the slang term 'anorak'. You might expect kids to love sports stats, but in baseball even the intellectuals eulogize about them – get them talking about baseball averages, and even the grandest men of letters sound a bit loopy.

But despite the devotion to baseball statistics, few people paused to ask whether they were studying the right ones. They kept piling more and more elegant brickwork on to the same faulty foundations. It was a classic example of an amazingly sophisticated system looking at the wrong information – a science lab using modern elite timepieces to record experiments performed with 1950s' Bunsen burners.

Then came the left-field revolution. A 'new' statistical system was devised by a baseball maverick called Bill James and implemented by the Oakland Athletics. It stopped generalizing about large chunks of the game that were too complex to analyse statistically with any accuracy. 'Runs' (which due to their scarcity are obviously more analogous to soccer goals than cricket runs) are big and unwieldy statistical subjects. 'Getting on base', essentially scoring a quarter of a run, turned out to be a more useful unit.

These different statistical measures led to different analytical conclusions: batters won matches to a far greater degree than had been previously considered. Many batters were also much cheaper than the equivalent quality of pitcher. In other words, the As discovered a market inefficiency – and baseball was about to rethink its oldest beliefs.

'Knowing what to measure and how to measure it makes a complicated world less so,' the economist Steven Levitt wrote in *Freakonomics*. 'If you learn how to look at data in the right way, you can explain riddles that otherwise might have seemed impossible.'

The As did to baseball what derivatives traders did to the financial markets. They broke the game up into tiny pieces with more precise outcomes – and struck gold by exploiting market inefficiencies in exactly the same way as traders had done in the '90s.

People argued that all the As had done was use James's theoretical ideas in a real ball club. But the more impressive thing was that the As were brave enough not to listen to the 'expert' insiders who proclaimed they were mad. In 2002, the As won 103 games in the regular season, more than anyone else, including the clubs with three times the cash. One of the As' guiding principles was: read the scores, not the press.

The As' successes had also challenged the theory that unbalanced wage distribution inevitably causes problems of competitive balance. They didn't have much money and they still won. The problem, the As would have said to the modern-day proponents of a 'reserve clause', isn't that most clubs lack money, it is that they lack insight.

But there is a less appealing strand to *Moneyball* thinking, and I would argue a wrong-headed one. Near the end of *Moneyball*, the As' manager Billy Beane scoffs at the idea that loyalty to players has much part in organizing a squad. You must know every player's precise value in dollars and be ready to trade even a high-performing and loyal player if the price is right.

In Beane's mind, his players are devices for getting on base. It is as simple as that. They are cogs in his statistical wheel. The less sentimental attachment you feel for them the better: your judgement should be led by a statistical assessment of market value. It should never be clouded by anything dangerous like emotions.

Moneyball is provocative and dazzling. But I remember first reading it in 2003 and suspecting that Beane's approach might have some flaws over the longer term. Players are people, not machines. If you overstress the centrality of utility at all times, people may start to feel dehumanized. Beane was right not to indulge his players, but wrong to downgrade them to machines in his own mind, and even more wrong to reveal his hand as he did so.

The book is such a great story, and the ideas behind it so intriguing, that I wanted Beane's team to do well. But in his dismissive attitude to player loyalty, and obsession with the truth of the free market, I felt he had overstated his case. If principles are taken too far they start to turn in on themselves. Beane's independent thinking had been revolutionary, but he was in danger of having undue faith in his own mantra.

Since the publication of *Moneyball*, the Oakland As, though still consistently high achievers in the regular season, haven't maintained their form of 2002; nor have they converted good seasons into World Championships. They may have suffered from imitation. Other, richer teams like the Boston Red Sox have applied *Moneyball* methods while also backing them with more cash.

But a deeper factor in the As' levelling-off might be that ultra-rationality has a downside. Throughout *Moneyball*, Beane and Lewis mock sporting 'hunches' as voodoo irrationality. But, ultimately, perhaps sport's human dimension, its romantic core, was being starved in Beane's purified realm of free-market values and statistical analysis.

Because teams are made up of people, not numbers or pieces of data, rationality can only ever be part of the story. The pendulum can swing too far away from rational analysis – after all, a void of rationality had initially created the scope for Beane's ideas and Lewis's story. But it can then swing too far towards it. And balancing those analytical and human dimensions is itself an art rather than a science. Put differently, every system, even the free market, has its limits.

Maybe managers and pundits should view statistics and markets as an enlightened politician might view opinion polls. He might well commission them, read them and draw conclusions from them. But the politician remains the master of the poll, not the poll the master of the politician.

Some economists would argue that we haven't really been discussing the free market so far. They would say that any given sports league – the County Championship or major-league baseball – may have various anti-market restrictions. But, other economists might ask, what is stopping anyone setting up a new, rival league altogether? Why should there not be choice about the governing body itself? The significant competitive element, they would say, is *between* leagues not *inside* them.

That is what happened in the cricket revolution begun by the Australian tycoon Kerry Packer. World Series Cricket (WSC) had its genesis in two main factors – the widespread view that players were not paid enough to make a living from cricket, and the fact that Packer wished to buy the exclusive broadcasting rights to Australian cricket, then held by the Australian Broadcasting Corporation. 'We're all whores,' Packer suggested to the ABC chairman. 'What's your price?' When the deal failed, Packer set up his own cricket series, secretly signing agreements with a host of top players, including the England captain Tony Greig, Australian captain Greg Chappell, and former Australian captain Ian Chappell.

Though Packer's WSC was banned from traditional cricket venues, he kept the league functioning for two years by using 'drop-in' pitches at grounds like VFL Park in Melbourne. Though he lost money throughout, so too did traditional Test cricket in the same period. Eventually, the ABC was forced to compromise. It sold the right to broadcast cricket in Australia to Packer's Channel Nine, which allowed Packer to dictate the organization and scheduling of Australian cricket. By the time cricket returned to 'normal' the game had changed for ever.

The legacy of WSC was enormous. Professionalism was here to stay; night cricket became a fixture; cricket was dragged, still kicking and screaming, into the world of competition and commercialism; coloured clothing and a heightened sense of theatre helped bring back the crowds; innovations like Twenty20 would have been unimaginable without Packer. Above all, cricket was forced to re-examine its deepest convictions. So it is with some legitimacy that Packer could claim his involvement in WSC as 'half-philanthropic'. Cricket has no Curt Flood, but it does have Kerry Packer.

In baseball, inevitably, the challenges to the ruling class came much earlier in the game's history. The founding organization was the National League, which remained the sport's elite body until the former newspaperman Ban Johnson announced in 1901 that his rival 'American' League was now also a 'major league'. He was right. The American League has survived alongside the National League ever since. This dual element has led to quirks in rules and customs. In the American League, to make offensive teams more dynamic, a 'designated hitter' bats instead of the pitcher. In the National League, where everyone bats and everyone fields, no such innovation was allowed.

In 1913, a new group of wealthy businessmen attempted to get in on the baseball action by founding the Federal League. This one failed, but the precedent stuck. Competition between competitions was up and running already. Baseball's free market anticipated cricket's by the small matter of about eighty years.

How about those baseball owners in 1879? We know they were wrong about freer trading being bad for players. When it arrived, in the form of free agency, it brought sportsmen a financial security they had never even dreamed about.

But were the owners right about the free labour market being bad for sport? Certainly, many people argue competitive balance is threatened by today's arrangements. From 1997 to 2000, the New York Yankees – owned by the ship-builder George Steinbrenner – won four World Championships in five years. And Chelsea, having been bought for £60 million in June 2003 by the Russian billionaire Roman Abramovich, won consecutive Premierships in 2004/5 and 2005/6.

Are the small teams getting a fair shot at success? As one of the things we love about sport is not knowing the outcome beforehand, surely those elitist trends, continued on the same trajectory, would damage the health of sports?

That might turn out to be true, and competitive balance may become an increasing problem in modern sport. But you cannot curb it, as the owners of 1879 tried to do, by limiting the right of players to negotiate contracts freely.

Don't take my word for that. Ronald Coase won the 1991 Nobel Prize in economics for explaining it. One definition of Coase's Theorem is: 'When there are no transaction costs the assignment of legal rights has no effect upon the allocation of resources among economic enterprises.'

That might not clinch the argument for everyone (especially me). So if that isn't enough to talk you out of hating Chelsea or the Yankees, or you need further convincing that high salaries aren't ruining sport, another economist, Simon Rottenberg, put it like this in 1956: 'A market in which freedom is limited by a reserve clause such as that which now governs the baseball labor market distributes players among teams about as a free market would.'

In other words, the reserve clause didn't dramatically restrict player movement after all. Nor did it help baseball by sustaining competitive balance. It merely restricted player wages. Big clubs got the talent one way or another, as the Yankees dynasty of the 1950s proved, even operating under a reserve clause. The only difference is that the players weren't consulted or remunerated as they were shunted around like pieces of property.

A far bigger factor in competitive balance – or imbalance – is the nature of the sport itself. In *The Wages of Wins*, a group of economists measured the level of competitive balance in fifteen sports leagues from five different sports from 1901 to 2005.

They found that, within each sport, the average level of competitive balance is quite similar. In other words, the English Premiership isn't significantly more 'one-sided' than the Italian Serie A or the Spanish Primera division. The Chelseas of the Premiership don't beat Watford with any greater degree of certainty than Barcelona beat the whipping boys of La Liga.

In fact soccer, billionaires notwithstanding, came top of the list in terms of balance. You are less likely to be able to predict the result between a champion side and a struggling side in elite soccer than in baseball, ice hockey or basketball.

Why? The evidence suggests that the strongest factor in keeping leagues balanced isn't lower wages or labour restrictions but the breadth of talent coming into the sport. A small talent base – meaning fewer players entering the game with enough basic ability to become great players – leads to a concentration of excellence at the top. In other words, with fewer brilliant players at the top of the talent pyramid, it is easier for rich clubs to scoop up all the talent. Soccer, on the other hand, is the world's most popular and accessible sport. Its talent base is the broadest, so its competitive balance is the best.

Baseball, though not as broad as soccer, has also benefited from an expansion of its talent pool. In the first half of the twentieth century, major league players tended to be white and born in the eastern United States. Now baseball draws players from all races and from across the country, in addition to players from South and Central America, South-East Asia, Australia, Japan, Europe and elsewhere. In 2000, 40 per cent of the major-league players were foreign born. 'The key to the competitive balance story,' concludes *The Wages of Wins*, 'is not league policy, but simply changes in the population of athletes the league draws upon.'

A broad talent base – encouraged by an unprejudiced and proactive attitude to recruiting young players – protects sports from monopoly. So the greatest challenge to healthy professional sports isn't the free market or high wages. It comes from computer games and the neglect of sport in the school curriculum.

8. Why luck matters – and admitting it matters even more

Sometimes it takes someone unfettered by morality to speak the truth. 'Give me lucky generals' was Napoleon's famous line about the guiding role of luck on the battlefield. He was right. Without luck, even the best plans can come unstuck. Luck is life's way of laughing at people who imagine they can play god. Perhaps it takes someone who really could almost play god, like Napoleon, to understand the limitations of human endeavour.

Many of us shy away from talking about luck. Which competitive person likes to be caught talking about luck – it sounds too much like wimpy self-pity? It is hard even to admit the guiding role of luck within the secret world of private thoughts: who likes to acknowledge the limits of his own self-determinism?

But luck is there all the same. I can think of at least half a dozen events over which I had no control at all that substantially changed my life. Whether or not they 'even out' in terms of pluses and minuses we can leave for later. The point is that each stroke of luck altered things beyond the stage where the path could be retraced. When the next stroke of luck intervened, it was a different life that was being altered. Our lives are not simply weighed in the balance, with good luck on one side of the scale and bad luck on the other. The journey, once altered, is changed for ever.

Sometimes that journey is altered very early indeed. In the case of potential professional footballers, luck may have played a decisive role in their careers (or non-careers) before they have even left the womb. The lucky child is born in the autumn; the unlucky one in summer. Why? A study by the physicist John Wesson (in *The Science of Soccer*) shows that the probability of becoming a Premiership football player is twice as high for boys born in the autumn as for those born in the summer. His explanation is that kids born in the first half of the academic year are favoured for school teams over their weaker, less-developed classmates. This early kick-start to their progress as footballers proves to be an enduring one. (I should add at this point, with some delight, that – with a birthday in July – I was always young for my year . . .)

What are the solutions to this inefficient distribution of talent? The football coaches of young children – at least those who think the national game is more important than the results of their under-sevens team – should look for the skilful smaller children who might be being muscled aside by less promising but more developed rivals. And parents especially ambitious to have children with a good chance of becoming professional footballers should take care only to conceive early in the winter to ensure an autumn birth.

More conventional examples of luck confront all of us who bat for a living. I remember listening to a colleague at university who was going through a spell of bad form. We walked around the boundary together watching another player making a brilliant but lucky hundred (all hundreds are a little bit lucky, of course, as I've never seen one that didn't include at least one false shot or a play-and-miss). 'Why can't I have some of his luck?' he sighed intermittently. 'I've used up the bad luck and now he's cashing in on the good luck.'

In his own mind, he had fallen on some unlucky sword of self-sacrifice. While the luck gods were chomping on his own cricketing carcass, they were smiling on the next batsmen and allowing them stays of execution. 'I'm just an unlucky batsman,' he concluded. 'Other people play and miss; I nick it.' Needless to say, he never came out of that trough of bad form.

Taken to that extreme, a belief in luck is obviously ridiculous and self-damaging. And wrong. Over the course of a career, I do think that luck in some sense 'evens itself out'. How many times have I been given out when I wasn't? How many times have I been given 'the benefit of the doubt' when I was in fact out? I am pretty sure the two numbers would be very similar. I don't believe, in pure statistical terms, I am either lucky or unlucky.

But statistics don't speak about *when* you get your luck. That is the decisive point. To be wrongly given out in a pre-season trial match doesn't matter too much; to be mistakenly given out in a crucial Test makes rather a lot of difference – to the Test match, and to your life. The important question is not how much luck you have, but when you have it.

Which cricket career has not been sent on a radically different course by one piece of luck? Which captain, having lost the toss on a day heavily suited to bowling first, has not cursed lady luck while watching his team get skittled?

The same principle applies to any acting career, singing career, political career, or writing career. The first book in the most lucrative novel series of recent times, the *Harry Potter* stories, was initially rejected a dozen times by publishers. Other authors of good books must have given up before getting lucky.

The book world, in fact, provides an ideal example of winner-takes-all chance. It is a metaphor explored by the American economist H. W. Brock. Imagine two books, written by two writers of the same ability, age and income. Each book has received similar reviews. Both writers work equally hard at their writing. Both authors would be equally 'deserving' of greater success.

Their two books are on the shortlist to be featured on the Oprah Winfrey Book Club on her TV programme – or the British equivalent, Richard and Judy's Book Club. (And, yes, vulgar though it might be for me to say so, I'd love to come on and talk about this book.) Imagine it is a contractual obligation that only one book can appear in the show – so a simple binary decision awaits the two books: yes or no. Let's say the book which gets on to the show will automatically sell ten times as many copies as the one which doesn't. The income of the lucky writer will increase exponentially. The loser gets nothing. Quite simply, there is no resolution of this situation without an acknowledgement of luck.

(Brock's thesis went on to demonstrate that in such a situation the rational decision is for both writers to agree beforehand to split the difference – effectively paying out an insurance policy against the possibility of losing and getting nothing. Brock's argument can be taken further: given that life is full of similar examples of winner-take-all good fortune, the tax code should take account of it by being more progressive for elite earners. Tax, Brock would argue, is a retrospective insurance policy — a premium paid by the winners.)

Situations like the Book Club winner-takes-all recur continually in sport, business, education or the arts. Two equally erudite university lecturers might vie for one professorship — and the one who gets it achieves an instant boost to his reputation. Two equally strong players might jostle for selection in a match that may go on to define one's career. Two equally good actors audition for a part which will turn one of them into an overnight star. The fascination of watching the repercussions of such decisions lies behind the success of reality TV shows such as *Pop Idol* and *The Apprentice*.

Despite all this, why are we so reluctant to acknowledge the role of luck? Why don't we speak up indignantly when we hear bland rubbish along the lines of 'You can be anything you wish to be if you really *want* it enough'? Why do we allow delusions of self-determination — and accompanying denials of luck — to persist?

First, we all hate excuses (or at least we all claim to hate excuses). Blaming bad luck is an unproductive way to live and tedious for our friends. Sports psychologists tell us to 'control the controllables' and scarcely even to cast a curious glance in the direction of team selection, destiny, fate or any of the other small issues that might come between our ambitions and life's realities.

But blaming luck to the point of self-pity is quite a different thing from simply acknowledging it. Steve Waugh, thought to be among the toughest and most ruthless of modern sportsmen, constantly uses the phrase 'lady luck' in his books. Napoleon, surely, would have approved. A correct analysis of why things happen certainly needn't trip over into believing yourself pitiably helpless.

Believing that 'you can be whatever you want to be', on the other hand, is actually rather an easy doctrine. (At least until you realize the idea has led you up the garden path.) The fallacy that desire and determination hold the keys to all success appeals to the inner adolescent in us that cannot bear the thought of hard work going to waste. I try, ergo I succeed; the world is just, so I will prevail; there is a fair distribution of justice, so I will be lauded. Such a shame it isn't true.

Of course, that logic is not reversible. Sitting around waiting for luck to come your way is as misguided as thinking that good things always come to those who 'want it enough'. The truth is that determination and desire are necessary but not sufficient. We have to try like crazy; we have to retain a relentless sense of determination; we have to make sacrifices and take the road less travelled. And yet still there are no guarantees. Even after all that, we may come up empty-handed. That is the bleak but unavoidable logic of anyone who has deep ambitions.

The relentless effort buys us something, but it isn't a deserving slice of the prize. It is a lottery ticket. If someone has great ability and great determination – then the odds of the lottery ticket coming good are obviously high. But safe bets still go wrong – just as long shots sometimes win. It is a lottery ticket all the same.

Perhaps people hold back from articulating this truth out of fear. They are scared what that logic may do to their own ambitions. Perhaps their ambitions would wither without the self-determination fallacy? Would people still get out of bed and throw themselves at the challenge ahead – even with their eyes fully open to the possibility of failure? Maybe not. People may like to play the lottery; but they don't like the idea that their own life has its own inbuilt lottery.

Maybe other perspectives are equally biased towards preserving the myth that we are perfectly in control of our own destinies. Perhaps those in positions of responsibility are afraid that acknowledging luck may lessen their power of persuasion. 'We train hard because training hard always works' is a more powerful slogan than 'We train hard because it is all we can control but doesn't give any guarantee of success.' But it is less true.

A belief in luck also strikes against the very popular social and political trend towards meritocracy – or, more accurately put, paying lip service to meritocracy. Everyone is now a 'meritocrat', whatever that may mean. Imagine a politician saying, 'I don't believe in meritocracy.' He would be lynched. It would be like saying he believed in the divine right of kings, or theocracy, or aristocracy. Yet many, perhaps, are meritocrats in style but not substance, saying though not really believing that society does (or should, or will one day) hand out opportunities perfectly on the basis of merit.

After all, can such a world ever exist? If two equally qualified people go for a job interview and one gets the job because his smile appeals to the employer, what can be done about it? You can appoint committees to investigate such 'injustices' ad infinitum – but who will cast an objective eye over the committees set up to judge the objectivity of the previous committee? How can we ever fully protect ourselves against the role of chance – chance attractions, chance meetings, chance human connections – interfering with a decision-making process? We can try; but can we fully succeed?

Of course, some societies, committees and systems are fairer than others. That goes without saying. But we will never arrive at the perfect world. Just as even the most high-minded judgements will always have a degree of subjectivity, so too luck will always be a rogue element in human destiny.

So to put a retrospective 'meritocratic' spin on your own success is always unhistorical and usually self-regarding – 'Achieved it all on my own, you know.' Dickens aptly mocked that in *Hard Times* in 1854 in his caricature of Josiah Bounderby, a fraud who styled himself as a self-made man. What would he have made of the even greater excesses of modern self-congratulation?

In truth, which of us, with the mirror held up to his face, can say he has done it all alone, without decisive and fortuitous help from other men and mysterious fates? Acknowledging the occasional – but sometimes decisive – intervention of luck leads just as logically to modesty as it does to self-pity. So if we are to become 'meritocrats', let it be for reasons of extending opportunity to others, not congratulating ourselves. Seeing luck for what it is can only make us more generous in our attitudes – and more importantly actions – towards those who were presented with unluckier lottery numbers.

Perhaps that is why luck, by helping to suppress envy, also has a social function. Sociologists such as Helmut Schoeck have argued powerfully that societies ridden with envy are often undynamic and slow to develop. As Schoeck put it: 'The most envy-ridden tribal cultures – such as the Dobuan and the Navaho – do not in fact possess the concept of luck at all, nor indeed the concept of chance. In such cultures no one is ever struck by lightning, for instance, without a malignant neighbour having willed it out of envy.'

Obviously, if every piece of genuine bad luck is wilfully misinterpreted as malicious sorcery, there is going to be a lot of bad will flying around. Acknowledging bad luck, particularly in the lives of others, means that disasters brought about by pure ill-chance are not followed by witch-hunts for 'perpetrators'. And recognizing your own good luck, Schoeck implies, helps to take the malicious edge from any potential enviers.

But whatever the practical societal reasons for believing in luck, there is a more important one still: it is true.

9. Freud's playground: what do Michael Jordan, Richard Wagner and Rupert Murdoch have in common?

'The child is father of the man' – William Wordsworth

We have all asked the same question: what keeps the proven champion going? Where can his motivation possibly come from? Surely he has nothing more to prove?

Often that question prompts us to celebrate the resourcefulness of human nature. I remember watching an ageing Andre Agassi win a thrilling Australian Open final. We had imagined Agassi's career would be that of a dazzling showman, quick to tire of the grind of continued excellence. He had proved everyone wrong: the showman had turned relentless pragmatist, and ruthlessly got on with the business of winning trophy after trophy. Agassi's victory at Melbourne that night was the high point of what Simon Barnes has called 'Redgrave', in honour of the five-times Olympic gold-medal winner.

I've seen the same quality at first hand with Shane Warne. But two matches particularly stick in my memory, both of them very closely fought championship matches between Middlesex and Warne's Hampshire in 2005. In each case, Middlesex batted fourth needing around 300 to win. We lost the first and won the second. I got 55 and 60

respectively, not batting especially fluently in either case –
but I was out there long enough to see one of the greatest
bowlers of all time hunting for victory.

Warne was thirty-five and well past needing to prove
anything. And yet there he was – throwing his physical
skills and mental agility at the task in hand as if he was
proving himself all over again. Even when he didn't bowl
his best, we were conscious of his huge and irrepressible
will to succeed. (It annoyed me when some columnists
later wrote that Warne didn't really try in county games.
They couldn't have been there.)

Yet that same capacity of truly great players to defy
common sense also has a dark side. Countless elite sportsmen cannot resist one comeback too many. Michael
Jordan, having interrupted his basketball career by trying
(and failing) to make it as a baseball player, got through
almost as many comebacks as Frank Sinatra before eventually calling time on one final disappointing spell with the
Washington Wizards.

More tragically, for Muhammad Ali, whose matchless
willpower survived far beyond his skills, the end came in
the form of two excruciating defeats against lesser fighters.
Watching Ali lose to Trevor Berbick, Hugh McIlvanney
wrote in the *Observer* at the time, was like 'watching a
prince leave town on the back of a dustcart'.

But perhaps a certain type of champion – maybe the
champion *par excellence* – seems almost hardwired to seek
the final challenge he cannot overcome. Is that the only
way the story can end? Maybe the same principle extends
far beyond sport – to performers in the arts, politicians, or
players in elite international business.

The pitch, the podium, the boardroom – is the stage universal? And what is it that prevents great performers from walking away? Perhaps the answer is closely linked to why they got on to the stage in the first place.

In a series of interviews on Radio 3 called *Peak Performance*, I spoke to classical musicians about their lives as performers, in particular why they had taken up music in the first place. It was intended as a dialogue rather than a conventional interview. I had become interested in the similarities between sporting temperaments and other types of performer, and I was trying to draw out any parallels there might be between what I had experienced and observed as a sportsman and what they had gone through in music.

I anticipated many of the recurring themes – nerves, pressure, ambition, fear of failure, connecting with the audience, concentration, solitude, resilience and practice. But I hadn't expected to hear quite so much about one thing: childhood.

Some, for example, could remember the exact moment in childhood when they first stepped on to a stage to play music. Indeed, one highly successful interviewee partly interpreted her whole career as an extended exercise in proving wrong the primary school teacher who had ignored her talents – a twenty-year riposte to being snubbed as a child.

Another remembered excelling as a child at almost anything which allowed him to show off. 'Acting, music, cricket – the final vocational choice was partly just chance. If I hadn't become a musician, I'm sure I would have done something else that put me on a stage in front of an audience.'

Natalie Clein, who won Young Musician of the Year in 1994 and is now a celebrated international soloist, spoke insightfully about what inspired her as a cellist. A sense of frustration, the feeling that day-to-day living was inadequate or unfulfilling, led her to seek self-expression in a different sphere. 'When I'm playing the cello,' she wrote in her private diary as a young girl, 'I can express everything I can't express when I'm in my shell as a schoolgirl.' Performing provided an outlet for self-expression that normal life didn't allow.

The brilliant soprano Renée Fleming made a similar point about the performing personality in her revealing autobiography *The Inner Voice*. 'I was naturally shy – doesn't every actor, dancer, or musician claim a childhood crippled by shyness? – but if I was told to get onto a stage, then that was where I'd go.' Shyness promoted alternative forms of self-expression. Performing was a psychological mode as much as an aptitude.

If you want to catch the performing bug, in other words, being something of an outsider is often not a bad place to start. It teaches you not only to look harder and see clearer, but also to seek alternative means of self-expression. Just as tasting defeat sharpens competitiveness, being out of sync or feeling socially dissatisfied can inspire creativity.

I think it is often the same in sport. Many sportsmen of all abilities (though they may never think in these terms) discovered the rewards of getting out on to the pitch when the rest of their lives proved unsatisfying or unusually difficult. Sport not only distracted them, but offered psychological satisfaction and fulfilment that normal living couldn't give them. The worse the school week gets, the more you look forward to the Saturday football match. Which sporting kid has never thought: I'm so fed up with everything else going wrong, this week I'll make sure I have the game of my life?

The three-times Formula One world champion Jackie Stewart put it like this:

Ninety-eight per cent of my ambition came from a need to prove myself because I had been a failure at school. School was a painful and humiliating time of my life. It was only when I was 42 that I was diagnosed with dyslexia. It was as if a weight had been lifted from my shoulders because I had always worried I was thick. Once I was asked to read in front of class and I couldn't do it – the page was just a clutter of words. I started blushing and the other kids started to snigger. It was deeply humiliating. The desire to overcome that schoolboy insecurity drives me to this day. Being dyslexic has given me that extra drive to prove myself.

It is not just a question of sport rescuing children from academic insecurity. There is universal solace in a system that has completely different rules from the rest of life. Sport enables people to walk out of day-to-day life and into a different sphere. Sport, seen from that perspective, is like a stage – a parallel universe towards which a huge number of people flee from the frustrations of normal living.

An imagined sporting experiment might demonstrate

the point. Think of the same group of children playing on two different occasions, in two separate environments. The first environment is completely non-sporting, purely a social scene – a playground without a sports match in sight. The second is an all-encompassing game of football.

Who will be the dominant personalities in the non-sporting set-up? Answer: the biggest, loudest, cleverest and so on. Compare that with who will be the major personalities in the football match. Inevitably, some of the dominant people will be the same. But by no means all. Others, who were on the periphery without sport, will have come to the fore once you throw a ball into the arena.

Sport makes for different winners. It may well enfranchise children who are losing at the game of 'real' life. They can gain a role, a voice, an improved relationship with people around them. In that imagined experiment, sport quite obviously has the same participants as normal life, but different rules. And different rules make for a different distribution of social rewards.

Sometimes merely stepping on to a new stage unlocks a new-found confidence. Some children stammer when they speak casually, but not when they act or sing in front of an audience. Others have no confidence at all during humdrum daily conversations, but then have no difficulty in calling the moves during a rugby match. Some people are better at 'performing' – whether it be football or singing – than they are at just 'normal' living. The stage brings out the best in them.

It is often falsely assumed that sport is the natural habitat of life's winners. In fact, many of sport's biggest winners became sportsmen in the first place because it was an

opportunity to get away from the frustrations and limitations of day-to-day life. For many sportsmen, their love of
games began as a refuge. To those people, sport hooked
them just like the imagination hooked creative temperaments. We hear a lot about competitiveness and belonging
within sporting motivation, but less about sport as a means
of escape.

The most underestimated sporting type is the outsider.
Because sport is a clubby activity, we imagine sportsmen
to be naturally clubbable. But many of them are not –
even those who seem engaging, or are regarded as good
'team-men'.

Like music, acting and the imaginative life, sport is a sphere
of self-expression. It allows people to play out parts of their
lives which are frustrated or constrained in day-to-day
living. To some extent, that is a Freudian explanation of why
people play sport. Writing (in slightly extreme language)
about the relationship between high-achievers and their
dissatisfaction with the external 'real' world, Freud wrote:

Thus in a certain fashion, he actually becomes the hero, the
king, the creator, or the favourite he desired to be, without
following the long roundabout path of making alterations in the
external world.

Freud was writing about creative artists, of course, not
about sportsmen. But the principles extend far beyond the
artistic personality type.

It is true that we are very familiar with the narrative of
the misfit artistic genius. The discontented artist is driven

by early social exclusion to inhabit his imagination; that imaginative world inspires the art which wins society's admiration; but even recognition, which the artist has always craved, fails to soothe his psychological restlessness. That is the identikit model for a genius.

Richard Wagner, the artistic genius *in extremis*, was a perfect example. He never tired of complaining that the world was making insufficient efforts to understand his brilliance. Even when he was feted by princes, philosophers and socialites, Wagner always thought people should be trying harder. Not even Bayreuth, a music-drama festival built for and dedicated to his own work, satiated his egoism. He needed and expected more than that.

The formative isolation, in Wagner's case, had a double aspect. First, as a young composer, he rushed excitedly to the world's musical capital, Paris – only to fail abjectly and slope back to Germany. Meanwhile his petite bourgeoise first wife, complaining of a lack of money and excitement, provided little consolation. A psychoanalyst might make Minna Wagner and the city of Paris the two unlikely heroines of this story. By rejecting the great man, they refuelled the artistic genius which gave us *Tristan and Isolde* and *The Ring* cycle.

Romanticism actively cultivated this idea of creative isolationism – the image of the solo artist struggling to explain himself to society. Indeed, it was seen as an intrinsic part of the artistic process. To create real art, some Romantics thought, you *had* to be a social misfit. (A formulation, unfortunately, that many post-Romantics still believe has reversible logic: 'I am difficult, rude and anti-social – therefore I am a genius.')

Even Picasso, when he mocked such theoretical self-aggrandizement, hinted at a kernel of truth in the Freudian version of the creative impulse. 'What are the aims of the artist?' Picasso asked. 'Fame, money and beautiful lovers,' he quipped. But if that were the whole story, why go on with the art when the fame, money and beautiful lovers are secured in perpetuity?

To creative temperaments, the imagination, once inhabited, makes living merely in the 'real' world seem bland. Many great talents continue to create, even obviously lesser work, long after their great achievements have been recognized. Only a few – E. M. Forster just stopped writing novels in middle age, Barry John gave up rugby at twenty-seven – can simply walk away in mid-career. Once summoned, 'the hunger of imagination', as Samuel Johnson called it, is hard to satiate. Retreating back into normal life sometimes proves harder than escaping it once had been. The path between the real life and the imaginative life is not always two-way traffic.

We are used to the idea that artists have eccentric and unresolved personal histories. But maybe other types of high-achievers are simply better at hiding that insoluble restlessness and its psychological causes. They may look and sound like what we take to be normal (perhaps only because in their world there has been no tradition of Beethoven-style behaviour to play up to) while really being equally psychologically distinctive.

Consider elite business. Not many international tycoons, however much the idea might appeal to them in the abstract, slide silently away into a happy and anonymous Tuscan retirement. They would miss the game too much. Hence the boardroom battles of big business continue to enthral the alpha businessman long after the issue of a mere handful of millions makes any difference either way.

As I write, Rupert Murdoch, at the age of seventy-four, has just launched a bold new internet-based strategy for News Corporation. Meanwhile Sumner Redstone, the 82-year-old boss of Viacom, has just outmanoeuvred his rivals at NBC Universal, and snatched away the prize of Dream-Works SRK film studio for $1.6 billion.

These men, this type, find it hard to know how else to live. The game itself has become part of the result. It is no surprise, therefore, that business tycoons and champion sportsmen (like Kerry Packer and Shane Warne) often become friends and share an intuitive understanding. The bonds between them transcend mere wealth, fame and pressure. In a psychological sense, they are playing the same game.

What drives high-achievers relentlessly on, when any normal person would be exhausted? Perhaps the answer is that the original spur never disappears. I suspect the Freudian theory of discontentment and achievement applies to other spheres of excellence. High-achievers, like Pavlov's dogs, keep coming back for more. Scratching where the itch once was remains irresistible even when the itch itself has gone.

For high-achievers of all persuasions, the means can become ends in themselves. To many great performers, the stage – whether it is the cricket pitch or the conductor's podium – continues to make normal living look pallid long after their reputation has been fully established. Perhaps that is why so many performers cling on to the stage even when their aptitude begins to slide.

To invent two words, *well-adjusted-ness* and *champion-ness* seem very rarely to co-exist. The well-adjusted man might well walk away when he is at the top, but how many of them ever reach that level in the first place? The champion, to repeat what McIlvanney wrote about Muhammad Ali, all too often leaves town on the back of a dustcart – precisely because the same spirit that first drove him to success subsequently blinded his judgement about when to quit.

We have entered the rarefied territory of arguably the greatest sportsman of all time. But the same principles, less extremely manifested, apply to the ageing amateur Sunday footballer who cannot hang up his boots – even though he can't walk on Mondays and scarcely sees his wife at the weekend. It is the simple, wilful child in him that cannot grow up. The strength of that childlike inner voice, to borrow from Renée Fleming's title, determines how long the sportsman keeps fighting.

One final parallel is that Freud made a similar point about the creative temperament. He believed it was a condition of immaturity. Creativity was an irrational state of mind, Freud believed, which its sufferers should eventually transcend. A properly adjusted grown-up wouldn't bother with the imagination. (By his own logic, a more properly adjusted Freud wouldn't have bothered to think up his own theory in the first place.)

What, then, would Freud have made of sport, with its capricious and ridiculous swings of fortune? What is any well-adjusted adult doing indulging the idea that such an outrageous world could possibly matter? It is certainly true that sport mocks too much rational analysis. A lucky bounce and the year is a triumph; a bad decision and a career is ruined.

That is not a place for cold-hearted rationalists. Perhaps it is a world where you have to keep alive – increasingly masked, maybe, but present nonetheless – what Freud might have called an inner core of childishness. If you grow up too much, you can't go on.

10. When is cheating really cheating?

Robert Tyre Jones, Jr was the greatest amateur golfer of any era. He entered only twenty-one golf tournaments and won thirteen of them. But it is for his sportsmanship that he is most remembered. In the playoff of the 1925 US Open, he nudged his golf ball as he prepared to hit it. Jones called over the marshals and announced that he had hit the ball twice. No one had seen anything amiss. But Jones was insistent that he must be given a one-shot penalty. He subsequently lost the tournament by one shot. When praised for his sportsmanship, Jones replied, 'You may as well praise a man for not robbing a bank.'

Jones was a moral man from a different era playing a high-minded game. But not all sports have had a similar attitude to cheating, even during their so-called golden age. Jones's contemporary, Ty Cobb, who was about as good at baseball as Jones was at golf, sharpened his spikes on the ground before coming up to bat, shouting his intention to gouge the opposition infielders if he got the chance. 'Baseball is something like a war,' Cobb seethed.

It is often argued that cheating is getting worse and sportsmanship is declining. But one fact often ignored is not only that rules change, but also that conventions evolve. In cricket, not so long ago, most batsmen (in theory anyway) claimed to 'walk' – in other words, if they knew they had nicked a catch to the keeper, they did not wait for the umpire's decision. They 'walked'.

Only recently has 'standing' when you know you have edged the ball become typical behaviour in the first-class game. And yet in rugby, until very recently there was only one referee – the touch-judges didn't help with disciplinary issues, only line calls – and the odd flurry of punches among the forwards was considered all part of the sport's rough and tumble. In the mêlée, who could be sure who did what? Best to 'let the game flow' as it was 'all part of the game'. But in today's rugby, fewer punches go unpunished. Rugby, though no longer amateur, is a cleaner sport. The boundaries of fair play, in other words, are constantly moving, and not always in the 'wrong' direction.

Above all, sport is riddled with inconsistencies. You can break some rules with impunity (everyone does it, don't they?), but if you break others you're a barefaced cheat (what's the game coming to?).

Unpick those riddles and you get into interesting territory. When is getting away with it acceptable? And when is cheating really cheating? It isn't as simple as it sounds. There is a rule book as it is written, a rule book as it is played, and a rule book as it is watched and absorbed in the stands.

In baseball, hitters try to get advance information on where the next pitch is going by 'stealing signs'. Signs are relayed by the catcher to the pitcher, who then tries to deliver the pitch that they have agreed upon. If the batter can 'read' the sign then he obviously has a better chance of hitting the pitch. Stealing signs, so long as it is done with the naked eye and not electronically, is not officially illegal in baseball. But it's nonetheless frowned upon. In 2002, Tony La Russa, one of the game's most respected managers, accused Sammy Sosa of stealing signs. Sosa immediately denied it, much to the amusement of many former players and pundits. Why? Everyone knows it happens. And Sosa wasn't even cheating anyway. Perhaps he thought his denial had something to do with keeping up appearances. But for whom? The fans? The game? The players' union?

I was reminded of all this while watching a Premiership match at Highbury. An Arsenal player went to ground after a clumsy challenge. It clearly didn't warrant a yellow card. But as the crowd screamed for a booking or sending off, the Arsenal man theatrically made the most of things. Perhaps, by playing to the gallery, he could 'win' his side a yellow or red card, just as Cristiano Ronaldo is thought to have done against Wayne Rooney in the 2006 World Cup. The offending player even more theatrically defended his challenge.

The referee awarded the foul but gave no card. At which point the Arsenal player accepted a hand back to his feet from the opponent who had fouled him, who promptly gave him a tap on the back. I fouled you; you tried to exploit it to your own ends (and failed); I pleaded my defence case; we all knew what was going on; no damage done; all within the code of professional football, right? It was all forgotten so quickly, I wondered if the whole thing was almost a masque, a piece of theatre laid on for the crowd.

And before we cricketers assume the moral high ground, we should look at our own track record. We know full well that the Edwardian public schoolboy was brought up to believe that he must be whiter than white on the cricket field. But few believe that now. It is a question of where the grey area turns to black.

'Walking' is a case in point. My father's generation of Englishmen was brought up to walk. I wasn't. But in one of my first championship matches, against Somerset (and Mushtaq Ahmed), I nicked a bat-pad catch and 'walked' – more out of instinct than morality. It felt out and I just walked off, almost without thinking. David Shepherd, the umpire, called me over after the game and said, 'Well done, lad.' Some in the Kent dressing room took the opposite view. The Somerset players didn't walk, they said, so why should I put us at a disadvantage?

Nearly all modern professionals (and amateurs, too) think that the current convention is not to walk but to accept the umpire's decision. The theory is that decisions 'even out' over the course of a game, and the authority of the umpires is upheld. One of the great passages of modern cricket – Allan Donald bowling very fast at Mike Atherton in the Test match between England and South Africa in 1998 – was prompted when Atherton gloved the ball down leg-side and was given not out.

But, under the same set of conventions, it is not considered acceptable to scoop up a half-volley at slip and claim it as a catch. A major cricket series is often preceded by one of the players, as Mark Waugh used to do, pleading that both sides accept catches 'on the fielder's word'. So it isn't cheating if you are 100 per cent sure you edged it but don't walk, but it is cheating if you are 100 per cent sure the ball bounced but you still claim the catch.

Like almost all professionals, that is the code by which I play my cricket. But I wonder how much longer the double standard can survive. There is room, I think, for progress – or regression – in either direction. It is quite possible, with more money and status riding on cricket than ever, that the convention will one day become 'do whatever you can get away with', as those two footballers clearly agreed to do at Highbury. That is the standard view about how cricket will develop.

But it isn't impossible that the opposite will happen. If the game becomes sick of fielders claiming non-catches, perhaps it also will re-examine its attitudes to denying the truth in other areas. Adam Gilchrist, one of today's greatest players, has resuscitated the habit of walking. Perhaps it will catch on. As Philippe Edmonds, the Middlesex and England left-arm spinner, has argued, 'If Australia get so far ahead in world cricket, they might have no option left but to think more deeply about how they want to be remembered, and how they want to feel about themselves.' Walking as a thing of the future? Don't rule it out.

Attitudes to cheating change imperceptibly. The professional foul is another example. It has always been a feature of sports such as basketball, where each player has a quota of five fouls he is 'allowed' to commit before being 'fouled out'. It is considered perfectly acceptable, and within your rights, to grab hold of an opponent who is about to make a certain score.

Such a view might seem anathema in rugby union. A good hay-maker here and there might be one thing, but premeditated spoiling of the game is surely another? Not really. How many of the great flank forwards, in searching for the one- or two-yard headstart, spent most of their careers offside? Nothing wrong with that, most ex-players would say – you play to the referee. But how about blocking someone's run in the backs? When the commentator and former player Austin Healey was asked what he would have done in a particular defensive situation during the 2007 Six Nations Championship, he replied that the defender should have 'run across and obstructed him'. There was an uncomfortable silence in the commentary box. It all sounded a bit dishonourable.

But what is the difference between defending while offside at a ruck – which stops the other side having the legitimate amount of room in which to play attacking rugby – and obstructing a centre in open play? Both actions limit the game's flow, style and attractiveness. Both could affect the result. Both are against the rules. The only difference is that the latter is more blatant. Is obviousness how we determine our code of ethics?

Arguments about cheating in sport revolve around conventions more than laws. It's not only a question of 'Was he breaking the rules?' but also 'Is that rule sacrosanct?' It is the unwritten constitution that exerts the stronger grip.

A case in point was the intense controversy that surrounded the Test match between Pakistan and England at the Oval in August 2006. The umpire Darrell Hair, as all cricket fans know, penalized Pakistan for tampering with the ball. Having inspected the ball and the actions of the Pakistan players, and consulted with his umpiring partner Billy Doctrove, Hair decided that Pakistan were guilty of ball-tampering and docked them five runs. Despite being in a strong position in the match, Pakistan were so offended that they refused to take the field after the tea break – at which point Darrell Hair removed the bails and declared that Pakistan had by their actions forfeited the match.

And so chaos turned into crisis. The match was abandoned, but would Pakistan also abandon the tour? Had their honour as a team, perhaps even a nation, been grievously offended? Could there also be a racist element to the incident? Had a sporting incident turned into a diplomatic crisis?

Much of the controversy centred around Darrell Hair and the sensitivity of the socio-political context. Had he simply upheld the law or over-exerted his position? Views could scarcely have been more polarized. Two of the country's leading sportswriters took up opposite and extreme positions.

To Martin Samuel, the fault lay all with Pakistan and not at all with the umpire:

Hair, we are told, has added to the volatile relationship between East and West. So, presumably, the next time London or Bali goes up, we can attach his decision to the list of liberal hand-wringing explanations for the atrocity. 'Iraq, Palestine, Israel, Lebanon – and that Aussie bloke who called Pakistan for ball-tampering at the Oval. Well, what did we expect?'

'All the Muslim players are sensitive individuals who are very opposed to terrorist activities,' Bob Woolmer, the Pakistan coach, said. 'To accuse Pakistan of cheating brings these tensions to the fore. I wonder whether Darrell realizes the consequences of his actions.'

What consequences? What tensions? Are we meant to applaud Woolmer's Pakistan team for their sensitivity in not endorsing mass murder? Are we meant to worry that, having been accused of ball-tampering, they now will?

Simon Barnes took the diametrically opposed view – that Hair was insensitive and officious, that Pakistan had been wronged, that times had changed. Barnes began by asking if a sporting event depends for its feasibility on 'the absolute unquestioned authority of the match official and the respect for his office'? His answer was 'no':

The culture of slavish respect for umpires goes back to public-school principles. Here, cricket was a preparation for real life: the boys were required to learn that they were there to serve some greater cause, i.e. the British Empire. But modern professional cricket exists not to teach but to enthral.

The umpire isn't there to teach us about God and the Queen and Duty and Service, he is there to make the show work. This is what Hair conspicuously failed to do that fateful Sunday at the Oval.

Within the controversy, we were arguing about lots of different issues which got muddled together in one unhelpfully large and intractable mess. So let's unpick and separate the threads.

Should umpires consider the 'bigger picture' before making decisions? (I'd be a bit disappointed, by the way, if an umpire gave me out when I wasn't because he 'saw the big picture'.) Can a team fail to take the field and expect not to forfeit the match? (No – Sunil Gavaskar tried it in 1981 and it didn't work for him either.) Were Pakistan actually tampering with the ball? (I've no idea, but I thought it was quite late in the day when we got around to asking that particular chestnut.) Should ball–tampering be legalized? (Possibly, though I'm not too bothered either way.) Can you successfully bowl reverse swing without ball–tampering? (Sorry, I'm just a batsman . . .)

Some of these debates obscured rather than illuminated the central question. To me, the debate was about the nature of the offence. Do we think ball–tampering is really that bad? We know it is banned, we know people do it, we know what the penalty is, and we have just seen the letter of the law applied on the authority of one man's judgement. But what about the offence itself? Does it exist within purely the legal realm or does it extend into the moral realm? Is it just an everyday kind of cheating (a not really cheating type of cheating) or the full-blown thing itself?

I come up against ball–tampering opponents quite often. (When the website Cricinfo catalogued the nine players most recently involved in ball–tampering episodes, I'd played with or against eight of them.) So, for the record, I should say that I don't want ball-tamperers to get away with it, for two obvious reasons: first, laws are there to be policed; secondly, if the opposition stop cheating it's more likely my side will win.

But I don't think ball–tampering ruins the spirit of the game any more than lots of other illegalities such as throwing your bouncer, deliberately scuffing up the batting surface before bowling last, or running on the pitch to create rough for your spinners. These are all illegal, and yet they have been downgraded by social convention to merely 'doing what you can get away with'. But Pakistan obviously disagreed. They felt that ball-tampering existed in a special category of illegality. They thought the penalty was an attack on their reputation as a team, even their honour as a nation.

As with the laws of cricket, so it is with the laws of the land. Are you a criminal? Of course not. Do you sometimes drive at 85 miles per hour on an empty motorway? Yes, but surely that's not the point. How about drink-driving? That's different, isn't it? That is a criminal offence – that's just common sense.

We do not see speeding and drink-driving as differing *shades* of wrongdoings but belonging to entirely different *categories*. They exist in separate moral spheres. On what facts are these distinctions made? Are you sure that driving while slightly above the alcohol limit but at legal speed is definitely more dangerous than driving too fast but entirely sober? Do you know the statistics for road accidents and what causes them?

Probably not. But you do know that drink-driving, thanks partly to effective government advertising, is seen as an irresponsibility bordering on evil. Being caught drink-driving is a cause of deep shame. Being caught driving fast, on the other hand, is perceived as merely unlucky.

Darrell Hair thought he was dishing out a speeding ticket. Pakistan felt they were in the dock for drink-driving. It was an argument about our attitudes towards the crime as much as whether the offence had happened in the first place. It was a disagreement about conventions, and conventions are always in a state of flux. Perhaps, in the heat of the moment, we could have reminded ourselves about that.

Conventions change all the time. Drink-driving has not always existed in a special category of motoring offence – older generations cheerfully drank four pints after a cricket match and then drove home. Speeding may go the same way. If one day we become convinced that speed, like drink, definitely leads to road deaths, we may not as easily laugh it away.

By the same logic – if a World Cup is one day decided by a ball that was clearly thrown – we may tire of bowlers who gain an illegal advantage with a bent arm. Conversely, if the ball-tampering rule is enforced often enough, it may become an everyday offence, just like a warning for too much appealing, or on-field ill-discipline.

As some crimes are upgraded in our imagination, others are downgraded. Analysing these fluidities and inconsistencies helps us not only to understand how often moral outrage is misplaced. It may also, with some luck, help us to iron out some of the inevitable flaws in our own personal codes of conduct. That is the nature of sport, and the nature of life.

11. What price is too high?

Bob Woolmer, found dead in his hotel room after Pakistan crashed out of the 2007 World Cup, had given his life to sport. As a player for Kent and England, then as a coach for Warwickshire, South Africa and Pakistan, he had thought more obsessively than anyone about cricketing technique and tactics. He sought to capture the game's deepest truths. He hoped that coaching Pakistan, perhaps the toughest job in sport, would enable him to add his own science and rigour to innate Pakistani passion and flair.

He couldn't. Unfancied Ireland, in perhaps the biggest cricketing upset of all time, beat them by three wickets in Jamaica. Woolmer, in the last images we saw of him, resignedly packed up his laptop on the team balcony after the game. The next morning a hotel maid found him dead. Whether it was murder or a heart attack remained unclear for months.

His death raised inevitable questions that reverberate throughout the sporting world. In the age of match-fixing and huge gambling, how dangerous a world is professional sport? What is an acceptable price to pay for the pursuit of victory, even an untarnished one? Do we throw ourselves at inherently impossible challenges? What are the limits of one man's cultural influence?

Some sensed foul play in Jamaica from the start, but we non-conspiracy theorists resisted the idea. I imagined that the huge physical and psychological burden had eventually taken its toll. Woolmer, we learnt, had type 2 diabetes and had become overweight. Pakistan had lurched from crisis to crisis – first ball-tampering at the Oval, then two star players failed drugs tests, then defeat and ignominy at the World Cup. Within sport, it is hard to imagine a more taxing set of circumstances for their coach.

Woolmer's death was deeply shocking long before it became a murder inquiry. In that first week after the tragedy – when stress rather than an assassin was in the dock – I wondered if Woolmer's death might make the cricketing community reflect about how much sport really mattered. It is one thing to live for sport, quite another to die for it.

Coaching Pakistan had visibly exacted a high price. I last spoke to Woolmer in the immediate aftermath of the ball-tampering controversy in 2006. Pakistan, having forfeited the game at the Oval after Darrell Hair had docked them five runs, considered abandoning the tour. But their next game, against Middlesex at Uxbridge, went ahead. Rain prevented any cricket, while a large media scrum watched both teams pad around aimlessly. I was surprised by how openly Bob spoke about his frustrations, and how heavy the toll on him. I had played against Woolmer's South Africa and Woolmer's Warwickshire. Never had there been any doubt about who was running the show. This time it seemed different. 'I don't need all this at my stage in life,' he said, shrugging at the generally confused and hostile environment.

So why did he stay at the coalface, away from his family and friends? What did Islamabad have that his home in Cape Town lacked? He was already acknowledged as one of the two or three best and most innovative coaches in the world. And yet he had stayed on the gruelling treadmill of international cricket.

No sane man could doubt Woolmer didn't need to prove anything any more. Sadder still is that we now know that Woolmer would have followed his stint at Pakistan with some much-wanted time with his family. So why hadn't he walked away earlier? Was the thrill of working with a talented side and within a complex culture too great a draw? So he didn't need it, and yet he did need it. How typical of a life spent at the peak of a ruthless high-profile world. The smell of the greasepaint remains intoxicating. Who can ever claim he finished at the top, and on his own terms? Peter Roebuck, as unblinking as ever, wrote that 'to a greater or lesser degree all sportsmen die in hotels'.

That people literally devote their life to sport is undeniable. Players often sacrifice an education or a career to make it on the pitch. When they reach the top, the pressures on them strain the deepest friendships and strongest marriages. Health and sanity are under constant threat in elite sport, in good times as well as bad. In 1961 Roger Maris, a shy, reticent baseball hitter from North Dakota, found himself on the brink of breaking Babe Ruth's record for home runs in a season. Hounded by fans and the media, he retreated into introspection, chain-smoking Camel cigarettes before each game and refusing interviews. His hair fell out in clumps. The better he hit, the worse life got. Maris broke Babe's record, but confessed later, 'It would have been a helluva lot more fun if I had never hit those home runs. All it brought me was headaches.'

Coaches and administrators must live with the added burden of being 'in charge' – they cannot as easily let down their guard or admit the pressure is getting to them. Many of the greatest coaches are performers to the core, more so even than their players. Carwyn James, rugby's tactical genius and the mind behind the 1971 British Lions' victory over the All Blacks, didn't just coach the game, he inhabited the lives of his players. They filled the gaps in his own life; without them, the emptiness was more daunting. He, too, died in a hotel room, in Amsterdam in 1983.

What cause did these men serve? They organized teams around the pursuit of victory. In doing so, they sought to teach young people how to make the most of themselves, how to compete, how to draw together. They felt – at a higher level – the same joys as the school football coach, the amateur conductor, the local theatre director. We all, deep down, fear the feeling that we haven't made a difference, and there are few surer and better ways of avoiding that feeling than by training a team to win sports matches.

At its best, then, the sporting journey touches life's noblest themes. And yet it is sport. Not quite life. We hope that sport, by exacting a high price in terms of effort and disappointment, leaves us somehow enhanced. But not too high a price. Nietzsche argued: 'that which doesn't kill us makes us stronger.' But first you'd better be pretty sure it isn't going to kill you.

Woolmer's death also raises questions about culture. If coaching sport is about problem-solving, perhaps the first question that needs to be asked is whether the problem at hand – coaching a subcontinent Test team, for example – is inherently intractable.

Both India and Pakistan began the tournament in the Caribbean fancied as teams that could win the World Cup. Both were eliminated at the first stage of a competition that seems to have been designed with the express purpose of maximizing the survival chances of the big guns. Both were coached by intelligent, analytical men determined to make a difference.

The case of India, though untainted by the overt internal warfare of Pakistan cricket, is just as daunting. The experiences of the last two coaches are revealing. John Wright, my coach at Kent before he took the India job, was a genial, resilient and respected Test player for New Zealand. In his four-year stint in India, however, the demarcations of his responsibilities weren't always clear. The captain, Sourav Ganguly, backed by the Calcutta power broker and board chief Jagmohan Dalmiya, seemed very influential.

Wright's replacement, Greg Chappell, appeared from the outset unprepared to let Ganguly run the show. With Dalmiya removed, Ganguly was sacked as captain, replaced by Rahul Dravid. India sparkled briefly, but failed to establish momentum going into the tournament.

If you don't tackle the situation, you risk it being someone else's show. If you do seize control, with Western methods and rationality, what is the cost to your relations with the team and the culture in which it exists? You might win the battle and still lose the war. Wright's India, Chappell's India – Bob Woolmer would have been acutely aware of these choices as he tried to guide Pakistan towards success.

How much, then, can one man – no matter how qualified or formidable – change a cricketing culture? Can he
shape a subtle, deep and complex sporting tradition? Can
he bend it to his own will? Not as much as we like to
think, seems to be the answer. Perhaps the task, in the
case of India and Pakistan, is inherently resistant to being
mastered – in fact, that might be its deepest trait.

And so to the most obvious question thrown up by
Woolmer's death: how badly corrupt is world cricket, and
how may that damage the game? The England captain,
Michael Vaughan, speaking shortly after Woolmer's death,
said his 'gut feeling' was that match-fixing was still preva-
lent in world cricket. Many rushed to assume that Woolmer
was killed by match-fixers desperate to avoid being exposed. There is no evidence that was the case. But though
the match-fixers had no part in Woolmer's death, they
remain guilty of threatening to ruin not only cricket's
integrity but also its future.

The frightening precedent for cricket's authorities to
consider is athletics. In the 1980s, athletics was one of
the world's most prestigious and glamorous sports. In the
mid-80s, I – like most sports fans – could easily have
told you about the world's fastest man and his 100 metres
world-record time. I remember the rivalry between Carl
Lewis and Ben Johnson, the graceful technician versus the
explosive force of nature . . . or perhaps I should say force
of un-nature.

The 100 metres final of the 1988 Seoul Olympics had
been the most memorable moment in my life as a sports
fan. Johnson, monumentally muscled and intimidating, had
blown away Lewis and his other rivals. He crossed the line

with such a lead that he took the last few strides of the 100 metres with his finger fully extended to the heavens. I'm so far ahead, he announced, I can celebrate before I've finished.

It was sport's most iconic moment of victory. Nothing I had seen had ever approached the expectation, drama and fulfilment of that race. Johnson had smashed Lewis's world record with a time of 9.79. No one will ever know how much faster the time would have been had he kept running not celebrating. Man was running impossibly brilliantly and impossibly fast – humanity *in excelsis*.

Johnson, of course, tested positive for anabolic steroids. He was stripped of his gold medal, banned and returned as a diminished figure (only to be banned once more). The tip of the iceberg had become visible. When an Olympic athlete came to dinner at my family home a few weeks after that final, my father asked how many sprinters were on drugs. 'Perhaps it would be easier,' came the reply, 'if I listed those who aren't.'

I've never been able to feel as passionately about athletics since. It is grossly unfair, I know, on those who remain entirely innocent. But with the continued positive tests, the exposures of Balco (the drugs centre of California), and the confessions of former athletes, doctors and coaches, it is hard to watch athletics without that nagging voice of doubt. Am I watching the best athlete, here, or the best combination of drugs and avoidance strategies? Such questions take the joy out of sport, and the innocence out of losing yourself as a fan.

If cricket matches become increasingly darkened by accusations of match-fixing, the same fate will befall our game. It is not skill that brings us to sports matches (though we may love it when we see it); if that were the case, we would enjoy exhibition matches more than competitive games. It is the battle to win within a context where the rules actually work. We are used to the idea that life is neither just nor knowable. Sport relies on being both.

It has now been confirmed that Woolmer's death was not murder. All the more reason, then, to hope that the tragedy may lead to re-engagement with some questions that are central to the relationship between sport and life: those who seek profoundly to influence a sporting culture might do well to acknowledge the limitations of their power; sport loses much of its magic when it consumes rather than enhances life; and when the ends justify the means, the game begins to die.

12. How do you win thirty-three games in a row?

'I am not equipped to manage successfully without Peter Taylor,' Brian Clough once said. 'I am the shop window and he is the goods in the back.' At Hartlepool, at Derby and most famously at Nottingham Forest, Clough and Taylor formed one of the great managerial partnerships. Within three years of arriving at Derby, they had transformed a Second Division side into the First Division champions. Reunited at Forest in 1976, Taylor and Clough won the European Cup in both 1979 and 1980 – an astonishing achievement for a club only recently promoted to the First Division.

They were different men with contrasting styles and gifts. Clough provided the charisma and star quality, while Taylor spotted talent coming up through the ranks. 'We just gelled together,' Taylor explained. 'We filled in the gaps.' In our age of mission statements and 'clear lines of responsibility', the concept of a partnership in coaching is out of fashion. Perhaps it shouldn't be.

I was reminded of the Clough–Taylor phenomenon as I watched a far less famous coaching partnership achieve equally extraordinary results. The partners are Nathan Leamon and Graeme Gales, who coached the Tonbridge School rugby 1st XV to three consecutive unbeaten seasons in 2004, 2005 and 2006 – that is thirty-three wins in a row.

Clough and Taylor were working at the highest level of their sport of course, whereas Leamon and Gales were active at a lower level. But there are reasons for taking schools coaching seriously. It is at school where a coach has the most power – not only to develop young players, but also to shape a team. Schoolchildren are inevitably more receptive and compliant than a bunch of strong-willed, established professional sportsmen. Good coaching skills and systems may help a professional team; they will almost certainly improve a school team. In other words, schools coaching may not be easier in a straightforward sense – all coaching has different challenges – but it is more revealing. American high-school coaches carry around with them a career track record and are often recruited from youth sport into more high-profile leagues.

Even in our less analytically rigorous culture, many of the great managers initially coached at school level. The Welsh patriot and scholar Carwyn James, that lonely prince of coaches, inspired his teams at Llandovery College, before leading the British Lions to glory against New Zealand in 1971. Just to underline the point he beat the All Blacks again in 1972, this time as the mastermind at Llanelli.

Alan Jones, the highly controversial Australian rugby coach and media commentator, established his reputation at The King's School, Parramatta, in New South Wales. In 1974, while he led King's to victory, he was talked about as the best coach in Australia. Ten years later, he was given the reins of the national team. He began with a Grand Slam sweep of the British Isles and didn't look back from there.

No matter what your view of private education, to any

serious analyst of sport the elite school sporting circuit is not a trivial irrelevance. In this age of league tables and free-market competitiveness, top schools devote more effort and resources to sport than ever before. In other words, when two coaches form a new partnership and within one year begin an unprecedented sequence of thirty-three wins in a row, it is worth looking at how they did it. As with Clough and Taylor, the partnership between Leamon and Gales wasn't always conventional or predictable. But it worked.

Before beginning the partnership with Leamon, Gales had run the team single-handedly. But he became a house-master in 2003 and no longer had the time to run the team alone. Leamon accepted the post, but only on the condition that Gales stayed on and worked alongside him. 'It was a novel idea,' Gales explained, 'and ran against the modern tendency – in sport, business or whatever – to jettison the old guard. When you jettison the old guard you are also jettisoning a lot of experience.'

Tonbridge had suffered a bad spell in terms of results. The 2001 team won two and lost eight; the 2002 side won six and lost four. So the turnaround was swift and extreme.

'I suppose Graeme was the artist and I was the scientist,' Leamon explains. 'He is very intuitive, whereas I am more analytical.' In their first season together, the 1st XV was unbeaten in the first six games, before eventually losing three games near the end of the season. As Leamon remembered:

It was after that 2003 season that I took several sheets of blank paper and wrote down every way possible that I thought we could improve. A couple of the opposition coaches had annoyed me so much when we had lost that I couldn't face experiencing it again.

Each of those small improvements leads to an accumulation of tiny advantages that you will have over the opposition. Innovations, tactics, training methods – they are like collecting cards in a card game. That's the metaphor Matthew Pinsent uses. You might not know if you have the best hand until game day, but if you can keep collecting cards, the odds certainly improve.

Unlike Gales, Leamon didn't have a strong background in rugby union. Having been born in Lancashire and educated at a comprehensive in Salford, Leamon was first and foremost a rugby league player (not a game for fancy theories or over-intellectualism). But rugby league is a famously hard game and it has left its imprint. Leamon, now in his mid-thirties and casually handsome in a see-if-I-care kind of way, has an unmistakable physical aura and presence. He speaks quietly and unassumingly, but with a certain confidence that isn't all down to articulateness or intelligence. Yes, I can handle myself pretty well if things get a bit nasty, his body language implies, but that's not really the point these days, is it? He is almost amused by that side of his personality – certainly not unaware of it, but not in thrall to it either. It's the light-hearted kind of toughness that you sometimes see in retired gritty sportsmen: really, I'm past all that macho stuff . . . very silly in fact . . . just don't push me too far . . .

Those qualities aren't always associated with having a degree in maths from Cambridge, which Leamon also has quietly tucked away. Yet I expect Leamon regards intellectual muscle much like other muscles. I doubt he would ever volunteer to bring up his academic qualifications. But if someone started patronizing him, I suspect they might not quickly forget the mistake.

Does being a mathematician help coaching rugby?

Definitely. I know how things fit together. Maths is about defining a problem and then solving it. So is coaching. People often forget the first part – each set of circumstances is a different problem. You have to understand the nature of the problem before you can solve it.

The school rugby season is a very predictable obstacle course – one series of games, the same opposition as last year, the same shape to the season. You have to peak in different areas of your game at different times.

There was a structural element to our tactics. If an opposition likes lineouts, don't kick the ball off the field. In the game against Dulwich, we kept the ball on the field for practically the whole eighty minutes.

The solution with the most elegance always appealed to the mathematician in me. I felt the same about practice. I used to enjoy working out how you could alter the relationship between skill development and fitness simply by changing the number of players doing the practice. We do one practice drill called the Auckland grid – four cones, four balls, a group of players. With sixteen players the 'work' to 'rest' ratio was 1:3, which was enough time to catch your breath and do it properly. With only eight players, they are working so hard just to keep moving that the skill development inevitably drops off. I find theory the most satisfying strand of coaching.

But he also allowed the group to evolve in its own direction, without over-prescriptive management. Sometimes Leamon didn't even know his own team's lineout calls.

As the week progressed, I liked to say less and less – to give the boys and the captain a sense that they were taking ownership of proceedings. By Friday – in a perfect world – I wanted to say three sentences, 'Everything okay?' to the backs, 'Everything okay?' to the forwards, and then 'Let's do a quick run-through' to the whole team. Of course, it wasn't always a perfect world. But the plan was gradually to remove my voice. I didn't speak to the team on Saturdays – that was the captain's domain.

You have to give them responsibility. An ex-army officer once told me he had never been able to work out why his men had followed instructions on night patrols so slavishly without bothering to work out where they actually were. Were they stupid, he wondered? Then he participated in an exercise where he was led, not leader. He quickly stopped taking an interest in the big picture and simply followed the guy in front. The army officer's point was: if someone else does the thinking for you, you won't bother to think yourself. As a coach, you are trying to encourage your players to think for themselves.

Leamon stresses the difference between being intelligent and being good at thinking in a sporting context. 'I certainly didn't think very effectively when I played sport. Especially cricket. I played dumb. I was a bowler and I had a temper. I used to think "You're not getting away with that shot!" So I'd get angry and then he'd hit me for another four. This made me bowl shorter and faster – and worse.' Leamon is warming to the theme of how dumb he played. 'I played dumb even when my body meant that playing dumb wasn't really an option. My back was ruined, but I'd get angry anyway. The result? I couldn't even bowl bouncers. Just slow long-hops!'

A touch, here, of the Billy Beane phenomenon? Coaches are often particularly keen to avoid repeating the mistakes they made as players. George Graham, a midfield maestro nicknamed 'the Stroller', was never too keen on tracking back as a player. Yet as a coach he presided over a ruthlessly efficient but unromantic Arsenal team. There weren't many George Graham-style players in the teams George Graham coached. So Paul Davis, one of his most creative players, spent most of the games on the bench.

Glenn Hoddle was English football's lost genius who played a sophisticated brand of European 'total football' that the English team never seemed able to accommodate. But as England coach at the 1998 World Cup, Hoddle sent home Paul Gascoigne and left out a burgeoning talent called David Beckham.

So do we think more efficiently about areas where we have ourselves failed? Leamon thinks so: 'Probably – one great pleasure of coaching is teaching the group to resist a mistake, even when they are naturally drawn towards making it. You can educate them to resist the wrong turnings that I wasn't always able to resist.'

Despite his laissez-faire streak, Leamon certainly isn't in favour of leaving everything to chance and talent. It is a question of balance.

You can be too over-programmed and cluttered in your planning, or you can provide too little structure. As a sportsman you are trying to make the right choices in game situations. If you've only got one option, it might be the right one – but there's a fair chance it won't be. If you've got a hundred options, you might have missed the opportunity by the time you've made up your mind. What you want is three or four good options in front of you – and to have enough confidence in your decision-making that you make the right one most times.

Sometimes people say just 'play what's in front of you' [i.e. trust yourself to be instinctive and uncluttered by planning], and I agree. But you can't play what's in front of you if you are fretting about whether you're going to catch the ball or not. It is having good basic skills that enables you to express yourself. The ballet dancer Nijinsky said 'technique is freedom'.

His co-coach Graeme Gales is more likely to quote Louis Armstrong than a ballet dancer. And, like a true jazz fan, his take on the unbeaten sequence was more romantic and intuitive. 'I think results had declined around 2001– 2002 because we stopped playing sevens as a school. Sevens teaches you to be creative, it teaches you about space and self-expression. We'd lose games because we weren't converting opportunities to score.'

It is attacking rugby that really excites Gales. 'I'm English, but if Ireland are playing England, and it is Ireland who are playing the more attractive attacking rugby, then a part of me wants Ireland to win.' There is no doubt that most of his Tonbridge teams played a very expansive brand of the game – but not, ironically, towards the culmination of the thirty-three-game winning streak.

The 2006 team didn't have the same incisive backs, so playing our natural style of attacking play simply wasn't an option. We had to adapt, which offered a different type of satisfaction.

We kept a high level of confidence. We'd been recording all the games and doing video analysis for a while – then we realized that if you put together a highlights package of the last game it was a perfect motivational tool.

We also found that teams were coming here looking not to win but for damage limitation – like going into a cricket match looking for a draw rather than a win. That played into our hands. By the end, we were winning games we had no right to win – simply on belief and momentum. The opposition were thinking 'Oh dear, here we go again.'

The most revealing aspect of both conversations was the way Gales and Leamon talked about each other. Obviously, there was great mutual respect. But that respect co-existed with a marked curiosity about the other's ideas. Phrases like 'You should see what Graeme thinks about that' or 'I'd be interested in whether Nathan agrees here' cropped up throughout both interviews. In fact, Gales's opening comment to me was 'What was Nathan's take on the whole thing?'

Didn't they know all that by now? What on earth were they talking about during those years on the touchline? Weren't their opinions well known to each other?

Obviously not. In fact, I got the sense that they never felt the need to iron out any differences of opinion about their sporting philosophies. It all added to the creative tension. Leamon coached the backs, while Gales led the forwards (you would expect it to have been the other way round), and of course they shared insights and tactics, but I sensed the vast majority of their energy was focused on the players. If they didn't always agree with each other on every point, what did it matter? So long as the team was benefiting from their respective positions, they were happy.

So there was not only a creative symbiosis, but also a balance of power. Sport, after all, implies a whole series of balances – between the individual and the group, between planning and fluidity, between conformity and independence. That is why it is misleading to think that one 'bad' system of thought is replaced by a 'good' one (usually your own). It is more subtle than that. The balances are constantly fluctuating, and always will be. You cannot master this human element, or resolve everything within a single brilliant system. As Mike Brearley put it:

One task of all managers is diagnosing the team's health. Is the team, for example, infected with a surfeit of selfishness, individuality, and pushiness? . . . Or is it, by contrast, one laid low with debilitating passivity, working to rule, and over-compliance?

In benign phases what is required may be conservative treatment, or facilitation – allowing people to continue on their creative and efficient path, refraining from unnecessary interference and change . . . At [other] times a leader needs courage and a willingness to fight the source of infection, as well as tact and freedom of mind.

In effect, the Tonbridge teams of 2004–06 benefited from the advice and insights of two team doctors – Leamon and

Gales – each with a different take on the group's collective health.

Through a mixture of luck and judgement, it was a perfect combination of talents, just as Clough and Taylor had been at Derby and Nottingham Forest. In one sense, it was obvious who did what and where the lines of responsibility lay. But at a deeper level, as with all partnerships, there was a mysterious element to it that resisted rational analysis.

Whatever the management consultants may say, with their flow diagrams and off-site management get-togethers, leadership is not an exact science. That is especially true of leadership partnerships. But anyone who doubts the power of good leadership need only read the score-sheets of Tonbridge's thirty-three wins in a row.

13. When Swansea feels like
Cinema Paradiso

When the Schofield report about the future of English cricket was published, I was finishing a championship match at St Helen's in Swansea. While the report looked forward to a more organized and professional county game, I sat on the concrete steps of a crumbling cricket and rugby stand talking to journalists about why our game had finished in a day and a half, feeling nostalgia all around me.

St Helen's has seen plenty of heroes. It was here, in September 1935, that Swansea beat the mighty All Blacks 11–3, the first time New Zealand had ever lost to a club side. In 1968, playing for Nottinghamshire against Glamorgan, Garry Sobers became the first man to hit six sixes in an over.

But these days, St Helen's seems like a Welsh setting of *Cinema Paradiso*. In Giuseppe Tornatore's film, a successful middle-aged filmmaker returns to his family home in Sicily. He left as an adolescent and could never face going back. Business, selfishness and ambition had all bound Salavatore to Rome; Sicily promised only embarrassment and claustrophobia. His long-overdue homecoming, prompted by the death of his childhood mentor – a cinema projectionist – is more than he can bear.

Why had he stayed away so long? Was Sicily more central to his life and success than he had ever admitted?

In my case, though my home was in Kent, a great deal of the family life I can remember happened in Wales, where my grandparents lived near Brecon. My grandfather – a Welshman down to his shoelaces – was happy to marry an Englishwoman but would not see out his days on the wrong side of the Severn. So they settled in the foothills of the Brecon Beacons, a long way from their long-since grown-up children and increasingly cut off from the support network everyone needs in old age. Granddad was a warm, romantic man – practical with his hands but not his mind. I'm not sure he even asked himself the question of who would look after his wife if he died first. But I am sure, as he whistled with the birds while walking along the mountain streams, that he counted his blessings every day.

We would go back six times a year, and Granddad would take us out into the natural world he loved. It was Granddad who showed me the different finches, picked wild straw-berries with me and spoke in awe about birds of prey. He made the landscape sound and feel exotic. Our walks had names – 'Where the red kites fly', or 'Where the bull gets his breakfast'.

The Wales I knew was not just about a Wordsworthian communion with nature. It had a warm social feel. Grand-dad was the unofficial mayor of the village, unable to walk past anyone in the street without stopping to exchange local stories.

Then there was the rugby. Supporting Wales – though I know it enrages my pure English friends who can neither see nor hear anything Welsh about me – was never a decision for me. It was a given. My father sounds as English as I do, but he went to a die-hard rugby school in Brecon, and he passed on that bloodline to me. Sport owes much of its romance to the oral tradition, and even as a cricket-playing English-educated boy, I could have told you as much about Barry John, Gareth Edwards and J. P. R. Williams as I could about Gower, Gooch and Botham. I wanted to be the Welsh fly half as well as England's number three batsman.

But my grandparents are dead now and there is nothing to bring me back to Wales. Until the week, that is, when Middlesex played Glamorgan. Appropriately, the game was at Swansea, where we had summer holidays on the Gower peninsula. So I pitched up to an old stomping ground to play an important championship match.

The Swansea cricket and rugby teams, now as always, share a ground at St Helen's, on the way out to the Mumbles. Between 1882 and 1954 Wales played inter-nationals at St Helen's, and as recently as the 1990s Swansea was still one of the most glamorous rugby clubs in Europe. But things have changed. The old concrete stand, facing the cricket square to the left and the rugby pitch to the right, is showing its age. Our changing room was so cramped that I moved out into the annexe next to the showers and loos.

The photos – black-and-white snaps of the All Whites – still endure. Before play, I studied each of them. There was Mervyn Davies, number 8, British Lion and Wales captain. He took the field forty-six times for Wales and the Lions, and lost only eight matches. There was Robert Jones, the brilliant diminutive scrum half, who the rest of the world reckoned was without equal, but who Wales routinely dropped in favour of plainer, bulkier journeymen. I remembered watching Jones's reverse pass against Scotland in 1988 that set up Jonathan Davies's epic individualist try. Rugby, as much as cricket, was what I dreamed about.

In the game of real life, Middlesex beat Glamorgan, and in quick time. In fact, the game finished two and a half days early. So the cricket ran out before the money-spinning corporate entertainment – planned for the week-end – had even begun. The pitch was poor and guaranteed a short game. As well as a bad defeat would Glamorgan suffer being fined penalty points for a sub-standard pitch?

As opposition captain, I was summoned to meet the pitch inspectors at the top of the pavilion. So I walked up from the dressing rooms, along the photo-lined corridors – 'No boots after this point please' – through the first-floor bar (two pool tables, wooden boards engraved with the names of club captains, and the smell of stale beer trodden into old carpets), up another flight of stairs to the club rooms at the top – where the presidents and special guests would have sat for all the big games at St Helen's. An elderly couple – the last of the club-tie brigade? – waited courteously for me to pass them at the top of the stairs. The conversations of previous decades – Was this new kid at fly half the new Barry John? Would you help us to fund our youth programme? – seemed to live on inside the walls.

I found myself torn about what to say to the pitch inspectors. What's the point in all these meetings if you don't tell the truth? But I also have a deep affection for Wales and Welsh cricket, so I had mixed feelings about Glamorgan – already languishing at the bottom of Division Two – suffering a points fine as well. There hadn't been any deliberate cheating or pitch-doctoring. But the wicket *had* been very poor – partly due to bad luck with the weather, partly due to the poor covers at the ground – and Glamorgan were eventually fined eight points.

It added to the melancholia all around – a crumbling old rugby stadium playing host to a sub-standard cricket pitch. It's all cyclical, say the optimists. But it isn't. Some wheels, having turned, never come round again. Welsh rugby, in the way it was once, is like that. Wales will doubtless win the Six Nations again. But the days when rugby was etched so deeply into the rhythm of national life will not return. Grounds like St Helen's, flanked by the backs of terraced houses, are yesterday's playgrounds. They speak of a link between sport and local communities that has not survived the professional era.

It is the social and economic context which drives even the great romantic sporting dynasties. Welsh rugby owed much of its grandeur to the circumstances of the country. The coal-mines provided the front row, the grammar schools the strategists and administrators, local industrialists the sponsorship and money. The mines, of course, are now closed; the grammar schools have become comprehensives; and local businessmen are now rather less keen to pull on a club tie and dine in annexe room 6 of the St Helen's pavilion (where I sat being interviewed about the nature of the cricket pitch). The glamour of sport without money has gone. Swansea don't even exist any more as a top-flight club – they have joined with Neath and play as the Ospreys at a purpose-built stadium on the way out of town.

As I write, the West Indies – who were as good at cricket in the '70s as Wales were at rugby – are 22–2 in the First Test against England, following on having been bowled out for 146 in their first innings; England made 570–7. No doubt the West Indies will have better days ahead, and threaten the top flight once more. But I doubt the world dominance of Lloyd's and Richards's teams will come round again any time soon. It, too, grew out of a unique set of circumstances. The English had gone as rulers, but they had left behind the powerful legacy of good administrative structures and a burgeoning sense of post-colonial identity. We need not praise the empire for its chance consequences. But the same social systems – schools and cricket clubs – which had previously been used to promote Englishness were very quickly and effectively adapted to suit the ends of West Indian cricket as it sought a means of political and racial self-expression. Cricket in the Caribbean, as we will see in chapter 15, enjoyed a perfect-storm scenario. You couldn't have drawn up a set of social and political circumstances more likely to promote sporting excellence. But planning had nothing to do with it.

It rarely does. Australia decided to turn around its sport after national humiliation at the 1976 Montreal Olympics – and did so. France, too, has enjoyed spells of government-led drives for sporting excellence. But much more often, sporting dynasties emerge organically. Sometimes the socio-economic ground is fertile; at other times it is barren – and no amount of money or wishful thinking will make the seed take root.

I was the last man out of St Helen's on Thursday. Like Salvatore in *Cinema Paradiso*, I felt personal nostalgia all around. I may seem very English, but Wales left an enormous imprint on me, particularly the sportsman in me. I draw more happiness from the casual warmth of team banter and affection than anyone would guess. I have a soft spot for practical jokes and exaggerated sporting stories. I begin many team evenings wondering what we will talk about and leave them struck by the sustaining qualities of self-mockery and a shared endeavour. All those traits, I believe, stem from my father's Welsh genes.

But the personal intertwined with a bigger story. Once St Helen's was at the focal point not only for Swansea's sport, but also a strand of society. Its glamour may never have been picture-postcard pretty, but it was real and compelling nonetheless.

What, exactly, has gone that will not come back? The answer is the immediate juxtaposition of elite sport with normal life. One of my favourite sports photos is of Roger Bannister on 7 May 1954, the day after he broke the four-minute mile in Oxford. An unprepossessing bunch of fellow students at St Mary's Hospital School have perched Bannister on their suited shoulders. His contemporaries – one still wearing a white doctor's coat – look delighted, natural and perhaps even a touch embarrassed. They know about medicine, but not much about the theatre of organized glorification. I doubt Bannister felt he was missing out.

A few levels down, I remember my first brush with moderate fame within the context of normal life. Rob Ashforth, my Cambridge room-mate, was the Blues' fly half. He was a prodigy, and played all three Varsity matches, sometimes as the only undergraduate on show. In one of his first matches for Cambridge, he played a brilliant hand in beating a strong Western Samoan international team at our old-fashioned ground at Grange Road. It was the featured match on the following day's BBC *Rugby Special*.

When we walked together into town that afternoon, it was obvious that people knew who he was and what he had done. That looked all the sweeter for the fact it co-existed with humdrum student life – the same books needed to be bought, the same appointments had to be postponed, the same lectures would be missed. Some things had changed, a great deal stayed the same – which seemed proportionate.

Driving out of St Helen's that day, through an unlikely gap in a fence, straight out on to a faceless dual carriageway, I imagined the huge buzz of a big rugby match there in the old amateur days. Those players would have enjoyed a huge local celebrity. But, win, lose or draw, they would all have returned on Monday morning (having tucked away their boot money) to their business, or factory or school – with a pocket full of petty cash, then, but more importantly a mind full of special memories within ordinary lives.

We should not always blame professionalism, or over-romanticize an amateur idyll. Much about sport has got better – and long may it continue to do so. But we will miss some facets of the old world, even as it disappears.

These days St Helen's seems like a relic, like the rusting machinery on that Sicilian beach in *Cinema Paradiso*. That is sad, but need not be a cause for reproach. It will come to every sporting stadium, and every sporting cycle. St Helen's has great stories to tell. Will our generation be able to match them?

14. What do people see when they watch sport?

Though I dislike the religiosity which swirls around sports advertising, sport does share similarities with religion. It is the broadest of churches with the most mysterious of liturgies. An intellectual could spend his whole life like a sporting Thomas Aquinas – believe me, there are plenty of them in America – cataloguing sport's appeal and trying to prove what makes sport great. Or you can tune out of the theory entirely and get swept along in the emotion, ceremony and sense of theatre. Scholastics or happy clappers – all are welcome in the sporting arena.

This breadth means that two sports fans may share an equal devotion to the game but experience opposite thoughts and emotions – even if they are both supporting the same team, at the same match. Sport's polytheism is part of its colour, central to its magic. We go to the same event en masse and yet absorb it uniquely.

There is, of course, an infinite variety of types of sports fan, and I could never do justice to all of them. But, in trying to sketch a few of them, I hope to draw out some of the major strands, essential threads within the sporting community.

I interviewed four distinguished, very different, sports fans, all of whom had achieved great success in another sphere. One underlying theme was: had sport informed their 'other' life? The second was: what part of their personality did sport latch on to? What type of fan were they?

One was inspired by sport as a metaphor for battle. The second saw the whole picture, more like the conductor of an orchestra. The third watched sport with the lessons of leadership in his mind. The last 'felt' the game rather than analysed it – he read the story of the match, keen to turn the next page. In the conversations with those four fans, I learnt a lot about the breadth of sport's appeal.

First, the sports fan as pugilist. Lee Amaitis, chief executive of BGC Partners and widely regarded as one of the biggest players in the City, looks quite a lot like Robert De Niro. He speaks with a strong Brooklyn drawl. When he looks at you, he holds eye contact with an unblinking gaze. If I worked for him I would turn up on time, never leave early and make as few errors as possible in between.

And yet, though his presence and persona suggest being at the top comes naturally to him, a big part of Amaitis wishes he was still on the trading floor, not set apart in his spacious management office. Using the first of many baseball metaphors, he explains that shifting away from the coalface felt like retiring as a player and becoming a coach. 'I was batting .300 [the benchmark for a good batter] as a trader, so it was tough to hang up my bat. I've got to be pretty good at management to justify the switch.

'Trading is a game, you've got to understand that,' Amaitis added. 'You're competing for every trade. And no matter how good you were yesterday, you start the new day at 0–0.'

That is something I have been told hundreds of times at the start of a day's cricket, especially if yesterday went well. But Americans, especially American businessmen, do sporting metaphors like no one else. Quirky ideas come from left field, the best of which they hit for a home run, maybe right out of the ballpark. Business, the saying goes, is the business of America. But it wears a sporting uniform. We are accustomed to hearing how American sports are run as ruthlessly as businesses. It could just as easily be argued that American businesses are run as unsentimentally as sports teams.

That includes performance-related pay and a clear understanding of exactly who brings in the big-match deals. 'That's the way the scorecard is kept here. You can't coast in this game,' Amaitis said. Throughout our conversation, he talks about moneymaking 'producers' – he was once one himself – with the kind of reverence that great sportsmen use to talk about 'performers'. That is the essence of the game: producing revenue, performing on the pitch.

Racing is an abiding passion. He talks about the legendary racehorse Secretariat as though it was almost a mentor. 'And Seabiscuit [the 1930s' champion horse which overcame being written off, ridden by an injured jockey and trained by the unlikeliest of heroes], well, Seabiscuit was a focal point for millions of Americans who were looking for some inspirational news during the dark years of the Depression.'

Amaitis has known dark times himself. The whole trading floor of Cantor Fitzgerald, the firm that was to be subsequently rebranded as BGC, was wiped out on 9/11. It operated on the 106th floor of one of the Twin Towers;

there wasn't a single survivor. He lost 740 friends and colleagues that day, including some of the people he cared most about. It was possible that the business would go under completely.

'I know for me the motivation was simple: I'm not letting these people – whoever they are – beat me. We're not going to lose.'

That sport can make a positive difference is central to his philosophy. Amaitis usually sticks close to the bottom line, but he does allow a hint of sentiment to enter his voice when discussing his time as an amateur baseball coach in New York. In the early 1990s, he and a trading friend took on the responsibility of coaching a team of Harlem street kids. 'It was rough but great fun,' Amaitis said. 'There was no grass on the field, just dust and glass. We had to donate the uniforms and gloves, which worked fine until one of the kids sold them. They were streetwise, clever, great to work with.'

There may be another reason for the emotional connection with that street baseball team. He, too, came from a tough neighbourhood where you had to be able 'to run fast or fight well – I could do both'.

Amaitis's office is covered in sports photos of horses, baseball plays, boxing bouts – photo finishes, stolen bases, knockout blows. Man as pugilist is man as Amaitis most admires him. So is there ever a time in the money game when the pugilists can suspend aggression and reflect for a moment on their battles? One recurring sporting legend is the post-match drink between arch on-field enemies – the scars inflicted, their respect won, the game over. Does something similar happen among elite competitors in the trading game? 'No. It's different,' he said. 'Business is business. There's no advantage in socializing with our competitors.'

Business is business – as if that explains everything. Sport is sport doesn't mean quite the same thing. That is probably why we need and love it so much.

But sport has clearly inspired and informed Amaitis's life. Battle is in his blood, but sport was not the right mode for him. Business has been. And throughout – the trading, the winning and losing, the tragedy of 9/11 – watching sport has reminded him about the qualities he admires and aspires to.

Where Amaitis lives at the frontline, locked in combat, Stephen Frears, one of Britain's best and most unpredict-able film directors, stands several paces back from the action.

Frears is a brilliant talker. The thought of being boring would be worse than death. So, too, would taking him-self too seriously (American). Or wallowing in theory (Germanic). He is curious about things you would not expect ('What is it exactly that cricketers *do* in the winter?'), indifferent about the familiar or the second-hand. I imagine he is quickly bored, hard to read and impossible to shock.

Frears also has the capacity to be vague while simul-taneously suggesting that he could be precise if he chose to be. That must be a useful skill. It prompts you to finish his question as well as answering it. 'I saw you were top of the something at some stage last season. Did you stay top of it?'

Hmm. Hard to say. Does he mean me? Or Middlesex?

How you interpret his questions probably tells Frears as much as how you answer them.

Frears's love of cricket dates back to childhood days spent listening to the radio from the age of eight. 'I started listening in 1949. I wish I'd been listening in 1947, of course, and then I could have heard about Edrich and Compton,' he said. 'I used to read the same books, Bradman's autobiography and Pelham Warner's *Cricket between Two Wars*, over and over.'

Frears knows his stuff. He talks about Shane Warne's performances in the 2005 Ashes. 'I thought he came across as the most wonderful man,' he said. 'Not only brilliant, but gracious towards others. And highly intelligent – that really came across.'

In his own career, Frears admits to failures as well as successes. In fact, like the best sportsmen, he faces up to them frankly. 'There are two types of Hollywood – the studio system and the independent sector,' he said. 'I failed totally at the studio system, and had some success with the independents.

'When I first went to Hollywood, I was searching for someone who knew the secret. No one does. You have to learn the hard way, and it's terribly humiliating.' Many top sportsmen would say the same. There is no blueprint for success; every journey is different.

Like an old-fashioned sports coach, Frears has a reverence for pure technique. 'The point about Judi Dench is that she can actually do it,' he said. 'She has the equipment to say the lines in a way that many movie actors just can't. A lot of it is technique. I used to say to John Malkovich [the lead in Frears's *Dangerous Liaisons*], "Can't you speak any quicker?" And he'd say, "I wouldn't know when to breathe." I asked why they hadn't taught him that at drama school. "I've never had a day's teaching in my life," he explained.'

In general, again like a successful manager, Frears trusts the people under him to do their job without too much interference. 'The people who do the technical side of films – the costumes, the sets – they are scholars in their own way,' he said. 'It would be insulting even to try to have a serious conversation on their territory. My theory is I'll do what I can do well – the human strands. Usually, the thinking is so hard there isn't time to do much else.'

Frears talks about making films in the most practical terms. 'Questions like, shall we put the camera here or over there? Two scenes exist, so another is required to link them. You are dictated to by the invisible structures within the film. The film is driving you just as much as you are driving it. You might be conducting some airy-fairy aesthetic conversation in your head. But you'd be foolish to let it out.'

I suggest that sometimes the best way to communicate deeper emotional points to colleagues is by not talking in abstractions. Stay close to practical advice and the emotional message conveys itself. 'Of course, of course,' he said. I can't imagine Frears begging his actors for extra heart-wrenching passion, as Kevin Keegan famously did as England manager during the final minutes of a pivotal defeat.

'You are trying to create a kind of benign dictatorship – though I use the term reluctantly,' Frears added. 'You are paid to make decisions, you can't avoid that. It's mostly about bringing the best out of other people. And beneath the surface, of course, you are dealing with the actors' unconscious, alongside your own unconscious – all on a day-to-day level. That's the Mike Brearley position.'

Film-making as leadership; captaincy as leadership – the idea obviously intrigues Frears. 'Brearley had the ability to be present and yet somehow absent at the same time. I recognize something of that in myself.' Perhaps it is one definition of the two-handed role that all leaders face.

Frears returns to a sporting analogy. 'What I really admire, and you see it particularly in players who might be just past their prime, is the feeling that what they have lost physically they make up for by seeing the whole picture. They grasp the shape of the game, they can somehow stand above it and see it clearly.'

When Frears watches sport, he clearly responds deeply to the player with vision, someone capable of orchestrating events – a Zidane figure, capable of expressing a broad vision in small and precise deeds.

'That's all you are ever trying to do as a director, to be clear-headed,' he said. 'When you're clear-headed, you can do it. There are periods of your life when you have that clarity. And then the fog descends again. And you don't know why.'

Throughout, Frears speaks in a kind of higher shorthand – nothing was unclear or opaque, but nothing was spelt out further than it need be. That would be a waste of film, a pointless chase after a lost long-ball.

Frears seems not even to hear comments that aren't relevant. His mind stays with his own narrative of events as he waits for the right opportunity to express it. The big picture is in place. It's just a question of the game – the film – falling into step with his vision.

Sir Rod Eddington, the West Australian who retired as chief executive of British Airways in 2005, combines some of the qualities of both Amaitis and Frears. Like Amaitis, he is down to earth and assertive, but, closer to Frears; he is also analytical and aware of the bigger picture. Perhaps those dual gifts hold the key to his own story.

Success becomes worth analysing when it keeps happening. One out of one might have been luck. A winning pattern, especially in differing conditions, demands attention. It suggests subtlety as well as self-belief, finesse as well as talent, self-awareness as well as determination. These are the qualities Eddington admires. Playing team sport, he insists, was a huge part of his personal development. Trying to win in one sphere – and sometimes failing – subsequently led him to win more often in another.

The idea that sport is a good training for life sounds old-fashioned – a Victorian public-school myth long past its sell-by date. So it is ironic to hear an Australian who led a British company talk about sport's educational powers without the baggage of class-consciousness. The New World, as is often the case, has been brought in to re-energize the Old – only to announce that the Old was on to something all along. That something is sport, in particular cricket.

Though he narrowly missed gaining a blue, Eddington played cricket for Oxford with Chris Tavaré and Vic Marks. Before that, he played for the University of Western Australia with the future Test players Rod Marsh and John

Inverarity. They both captained him and have remained lifelong friends.

'They set people up for success by creating the right environment,' he said. That atmosphere was confident, tough, but always fun – the environment, I suspect, Eddington wanted to be surrounded by at the headquarters of BA.

There is an urgency to his analysis of sport, which ranges from yesterday's Test match to his own playing days in the '60s and '70s. He talks about a recent Australian Test victory with a reverence for victory in his voice. That is what they are about, he implies, that is what I am about.

'I was a limited sportsman, so it made me realize what I could and couldn't do,' he says. 'But I was also drawn to the fact that the numbers didn't lie. Sport is unspinnable. You get that same clarity in business.'

Eddington dislikes the idea of having an inflexible business strategy. 'When I was chief executive at Cathay Pacific, I felt the best models I could learn from were other Asian companies like Nissan and Toyota, even though they were not in the aviation industry. Here, at BA, it would be foolish to think that running a business in Europe will respond to the same principles as running one in Asia.'

Axioms come easily to Eddington. 'Take good ideas from wherever you can' is one of his favourites, 'but don't expect them to work in a different environment without clever adaptation. You can't just take an old blueprint out of the draw, dust it off, and apply it to a completely different challenge. Rod Laver won on grass, he won on clay – he understood how to adapt.'

Eddington spent his first ninety days in charge at BA

almost exclusively asking questions. 'Most bad business decisions stem from a failure to understand the nature of the problem,' he says. 'Before you can work out where you want to go – let alone get there – you have to know where you are starting from. The bad coach jumps in after watching only a few balls in the nets. The good one first goes to watch from a number of angles.' Eddington is a curious person, a curiosity fortified by his understanding that before you can lead people you have to have formed a connection with them.

'There are two main challenges to business strategy – analysis and implementation, knowing what to do and then knowing how to do it. They are separate skills, and demand separate gifts,' he says. 'Some of the cleverest people aren't always the most effective at making changes because they are all analysis and less good at implementation.'

Eddington returns to his theme of how management often demands a slower burn. 'One common characteristic of very insightful people is impatience,' he says. 'But to effect change you have to understand that some colleagues get it straightaway and others need to be taken on a journey of self-discovery. You need patience as well as good ideas.' I suspect Eddington rates himself as only quite good as an original thinker, good at implementing ideas, and very good indeed at getting the right blend of the two traits. For that reason, with Eddington the whole is more than the sum of the parts.

Winning, having a good record as a businessman, obviously matters hugely to Eddington. But he doesn't have blind faith that he can overcome any odds. I remember bumping into him shortly after 9/11 – when BA was losing between £1 million and £2 million a day. His tone was that he was up for the fight, and determined to do everything to turn it round, but that it might be beyond him – an implicit acknowledgement of luck.

He was focused on delivering his part of the deal – good leadership – rather than grandstanding about how he would never tolerate defeat. 'If your self-confidence is based on faulty analysis, you are simply guaranteeing failure,' he says. Again, Eddington turns to sport to clarify his point. 'The culture of the cricket I played in Perth encouraged self-belief, but it never allowed egotism and overconfidence to obscure good judgement.'

Perhaps a sporting sense of fun and boyish adventure have also stayed with him. Constant travel numbs the emotions, even if you are chief executive. It is lonely at the top of a business empire, especially for those who are naturally warm-spirited. Even more important than the many business lessons he has learnt from sport, Eddington is most grateful for the enduring friendships he made on the cricket field. The battles may have receded into memory, but the bonds remain.

Perhaps that, too, may have informed his business career. How many captains of industry understand that friendship has a sustaining quality all of its own?

Nick Hornby, for all his creative intelligence, would happily admit he wouldn't always understand, let alone endorse, what these successful men were finding in sport. For him sport is far simpler, more visceral and primal. Life lessons? Strategic insight? What's the bloody score? That's what he would want to know.

It is a decade and a half since he published *Fever Pitch*, a memoir of his life as an obsessive Arsenal fan. It quickly became a cult book and launched his career as one of the country's most successful writers. More than that, *Fever Pitch* was the start of something broader, a tipping point for English sports writing. It was the first football book to win highbrow critical acclaim as well as reaching a wide readership. It won the William Hill Sports Book of the Year award in 1992, and Hornby's writing 'voice', intelligent but rooted in popular culture, resonated beyond literary circles.

'I have always believed in a unified culture – books, sport, music,' he said. 'In that way, I am probably quite American. To me, there is no contradiction in loving all those things. In England, we still have this strange debate about whether it is odd to be immersed in football as well as literature.'

Hornby's conversation is littered with football anecdotes and perceptions, but I get the impression that Hornby is less obsessive about Arsenal than he used to be. 'Yes, that's true, a bad game never ruins an evening these days,' he said. 'Following Arsenal did fill a lot of holes in my life – sport expanded to fill the time available.' Does a part of him miss his old obsessive days? 'The highs aren't quite as high now,' he said. 'But there's no nostalgia. I'm glad the holes in my life aren't so big.'

But he is still at it. After spending a large part of an interesting life watching Arsenal, he still shares their journey. Why? 'Obviously, a sense of belonging is a big part of being a fan,' he said. 'But when I am watching a game, the central thing is finding out what happens next. I've never lost that fascination with the narrative.

'I am pretty "switched off", in terms of my analytical mind, when I am watching football. I am a very passive consumer. I watch the game in the same way I read a thriller.'

Feeling, not thinking, losing yourself in a story over which you have no control, absorption in something beyond your own preoccupations – that's probably no bad thing for a novelist. It is also not too fanciful to say it might be a part of what has kept Hornby such an obviously warm person.

That might be one of the things people like about his writing. For other writers with an effortless vernacular style – the classic being Kingsley Amis – the clear eye and witty pen pointed to a cool heart. That doesn't appear to be the case with Hornby.

What does it do to us – following a narrative, sharing a journey, caring deeply about something we cannot change? Might that extend our human sympathy? That is the argument always made about reading. The 'lesson', such as it is, is in the caring not the message.

So is watching sport good for you? 'I'd need two weeks to think it over!' Hornby said with a laugh. But it's a nice idea, his kind of idea. I expect he might agree more quickly if he wasn't so reticent about anything that sounds pretentious.

But I think Hornby watches sport as most people do – albeit at a greater fever pitch. Perhaps many of us – and this book – rather neglect these quiet, serious, feeling fans. They are not the shouting members of the mob. Nor are they the aesthetes or strategists who take the pieces of sport and fit them into their own philosophies.

These fans are the type who simply trace the action and are moved by what they see. They follow the plot in their hearts. They may very much want one team to win, but they aren't blind to the sadness of wishing defeat on the opposition. They seek rather than demand victory, admire brilliance, sympathize with humiliation and crave sportsmanship.

They constantly find in sport new versions of old stories – the oldest and deepest stories of all. They may wish these stories would turn out happily more often, but they recognize that they never will. Theirs is a hope tinged with regret, a very human kind of hope.

They follow sport privately, because it seems true, not for the excesses of total victory. Many are women. Most do not have the conventional attitudes of the 'typical sports fan'. They are sport's silent majority. If only we listened to them more, it would make sport more rewarding.

15. Cricket, C. L. R. James and Marxism

It is said that great eras warrant great chroniclers. That was certainly the case with the coming of age of West Indies cricket and the man who immortalized it in print, C. L. R. James. Himself a fine club cricketer in Trinidad, James knew many of the men – especially Learie Constantine – who turned the West Indies into a major cricketing force. James was also a Marxist and social theorist, and his *Beyond a Boundary*, first published in 1963, used cricket as a prism through which he hoped to demonstrate his political ideas.

It is possibly the most ambitious and certainly the most trumpeted of cricket books. It is routinely described as 'the greatest sports book ever written', though the *Guardian* considered that 'pifflingly inadequate praise'. It is so often praised and quoted that many people never seem to get around to reading it. It is certainly worth doing so, though not always for the reasons you expect.

One of the most memorable stories in *Beyond a Boundary* is not even about cricket. It comes early in the first chapter, as if to illuminate one of the book's underlying preoccupations: the relationship between rulers and ruled. The tale describes how James's grandfather, an elderly black working man, mended a broken engine in a sugar-cane factory:

The engines of one of the big sugar-estate factories had failed. Whenever this took place it caused a general crisis. During the season the factories ground cane often twenty hours a day . . . If the big engines stopped and were not repaired pretty quickly the whole process was thrown out of gear, and if the break continued the cutters for miles around had to be signalled to stop cutting, and they sat around and waited for hours. I have worked on a sugar estate and the engineers, usually Scotsmen, walked around doing nothing for days; but as soon as there was the slightest sign of anything wrong the tension was immediately acute. The manager himself, if not an engineer, was usually a man who understood something about engines. There were always one or two coloured foremen who had no degrees and learnt empirically, but who knew their engines inside out. All these worked frantically, like men on a wrecked ship.

But nothing worked in this instance and they called for James's grandfather, Josh Rudder.

Everyone turned to him as if he were the last hope . . . Josh knew what he was about. When the manager invited him to enter the engine-room, and, naturally, was coming in with him (with all the others crowding behind) Josh stopped and, turning to all of them, said very firmly, 'I would like to go in alone.' The manager looked at him in surprise, but . . . agreed.

. . . No one will ever know what Josh did in there, but within two minutes he was out again and he said to the astonished manager, 'I can't guarantee anything, sir, but try and see if she will go now.' The foreman rushed inside, and after a few tense minutes the wheels started to revolve again.

An enthusiastic crowd, headed by the manager, surrounded

Josh, asking him what it was that had performed the miracle. But the always exuberant Josh grew silent for once and refused to say. He never told them. The obstinate man wouldn't even tell me. But when I asked him that day, 'Why did you do it?' he said what I had never heard before. 'They were white men with all their M.I.C.E. and R.I.C.E. and all their big degrees, and it was their business to fix it. I had to fix it for them. Why should I tell them?'

What follows in *Beyond a Boundary* explores this theme. It is a study in self-reliance and, to use James's phrase, 'empirical learning'. That means independent thinking and overcoming problems – learning cricket on the beach, not from the MCC coaching manual.

James's book is about achieving excellence in cricket despite being outside the ruling establishment and all its privileges. In fact, that is an understatement. It is about achieving excellence *because of* exclusion from the ruling establishment. It is about being the underdog, and how that can be more inspiring than being governed by the prescriptive rules of conventional wisdom.

Grandfather Josh – represented in cricketing terms by Constantine, Worrell, Weekes, Walcott, Ramadhin and Valentine – started to fix the engines of cricket. They came up with new, often better, methods. They did so empirically, naturally, sometimes instinctively. James liked what he saw and wrote the story.

What leads people to throw themselves at the challenge of sporting excellence – and what enables them to do it? West Indian cricket, James shows, drew from a deep well not only of talent but also of profound discontent:

I haven't the slightest doubt that the clash of race, caste and class did not retard but stimulated West Indian cricket. I am equally certain that in those years social and political passions, denied normal outlets, expressed themselves so fiercely in cricket precisely because they were games.

The conditions of life provided the spur. And the conditions of cricket – the beach, variable club wickets, an intuitive approach to learning – led to discovery and innovation. A will and a means: the combination proved unstoppable.

Constantine ushered in the new dawn. Then, in 1950, the West Indies won a watershed victory against England at Lord's. The Three Ws – Worrell, Weekes and Walcott – not only provided a top-middle order that would have improved any team in the world, but the later statesmanlike leadership of Worrell eventually took the team to new levels of organization and drive. In the '60s, with a bowling attack spearheaded by Hall and Griffith, they developed a reputation for fearsome fast bowling that endured for decades. Above all, in the happy-go-lucky personality of Garry Sobers, the West Indies found just the kind of fully fledged genius who adds glamour to any sport.

There was more to come. Writing in *Wisden* in 1986, the peak of Caribbean cricketing supremacy, David Frith argued that West Indies cricket had inspired the entire Afro-Caribbean people:

In the pre-War Depression years, Don Bradman stood for the powers of endurance of the ordinary bloke. His triumphs brought pride and inspiration to the masses of struggling Australians in town and bush. Through The Don they saw that life's difficulties were at least not totally universal. Spasmodically they too tasted success on a giant scale, if only vicariously. 'Our Don' took his admirers out of themselves, made their existences less wretched, gave them a kind of hope.

For ten years now Viv Richards has done something similar for the black man.

In that winter of 1985/6, England had endured a brutal 5–0 defeat on their tour of the Caribbean. An array of brilliant West Indies batsmen – led by Richards – and a seemingly endless battery of fast bowlers had once again blown England away.

Like most cricketing boys who grew up in the '80s, I came to associate both success and style with the West Indian team. The most terrifying cricketer in the world was Malcolm Marshall, the coolest was Jeffrey Dujon, the best and most iconic was Viv Richards. Even the most diehard England fan knew that the West Indies were playing a higher brand of cricket. They were the game's undoubted masters.

It has not endured. The Test teams of the late 1990s and 2000s have found themselves near the bottom of the ICC world rankings. Brian Lara has broken most batting records in the book, but without a team to match. There are countless arguments – as we shall see – used to explain the relative decline of West Indian cricket.

In December 2006, on the eve of the Cricket World Cup 2007 hosted by the West Indies, I visited the Caribbean, keen to gauge the mood of the cricketing environment. Speaking to players, administrators and coaches, I heard many theories about how to revitalize cricket in the Caribbean. More money, they said, or better infrastructure, improved youth systems, extra biomechanics experts, perhaps more academies to develop young players.

There may be some truth in all of them. But each of those theories, in their differing ways, proposes improving the means by which received wisdom is polished and then communicated. At its core, each theory is based on the principle that sporting progress is about efficient dissemination of existing ideas. First, learn how it is done best; second, tell the next generation that is the way to do it. In other words, the 'new' ideas may sound progressive but are in fact reactionary.

Is that the way the West Indies got to the top in the first place? Has any sporting culture advanced in that way? Perhaps, when seeking to explain a decline in fortunes, the first question should be not: 'What went wrong?' but instead: 'What made it good in the first place?' It is the same question in reverse form, substituting a positive in place of a negative. With many sporting successes, the most important part of the story was the will to succeed and the bravery to experiment. If those conditions are not in place, a blueprint for resuscitating any sport is merely moving round the deckchairs as the *Titanic* sinks.

The essence of sport can be seen as simple problem-solving: trying to get the ball over the posts as often as you can; trying to hit the ball to the rope as many times as possible without being caught; hitting the other man without getting hit. So the last thing you want in a sportsman is a reluctance to think independently. Sport is, or should be, always on the lookout for better ways of solving familiar problems. What was once considered 'not in the batting technique' – like the sweep or the reverse-sweep – two decades later is a staple means of getting runs. 'Why wouldn't you?' is a very good question for a sportsman to ask.

It is an unsettling fact (for administrators, anyway) that a high percentage of the greatest sportsmen learnt to play in an unstructured environment. They weren't over-coached at a young age; they learnt intuitively and from experience. Above all, they learnt to figure things out for themselves.

Cricket provides plenty of examples of legends who learnt their own way, without great intervention by a cricketing 'system': Don Bradman, Sunil Gavaskar, Len Hutton, Graeme Pollock, Viv Richards, Garry Sobers, Michael Holding, Harold Larwood, Dennis Lillee, Jeff Thomson, Fred Trueman, Derek Underwood, among many others.

I am not arguing we would all be better left alone to sink or swim. Many players have benefited hugely from coaching and wouldn't have got as far without it. I come from a family full of teachers – both my grandfathers were headmasters, both my parents are teachers – so I know all about the upside of good education. But the best teachers lead rather than drag. They provide the apparatus for self-improvement not a dependency culture. They instil a curious mind not a slavish dedication to other people's ideas. Above all, the best teachers teach independent thinking.

The big jumps forward in sporting evolution are usually taken by people who think for themselves. They are able to experiment within a larger range of options. They say,

'Why shouldn't I do it differently?' rather than 'It looks like other people always do it this way.'

That is how Josh Rudder fixed the engine. James was right to see it as an ideal metaphor for sport, right down to the old man not explaining how he did it. We can easily imagine the smile on Josh's face – wry, amused and enigmatic. It is the look of self-reliance mocking received wisdom. It says, 'Don't ask – look and think.'

How odd, then, that C. L. R. James should have been a Marxist. It is a system of governance, more than any other, which precludes independent thought and freedom of discovery. Right from the start, Marxism was predicated on an appointed inner sanctum of controllers. Lenin argued that since Marxist revolution is based on theory, and only intellectuals can understand theory, only an intellectual elite can lead the revolution: 'the educated representatives of the propertied class, the intelligentsia'.

Since socialism gives an administrative monopoly to one party, the party quickly and inevitably turns into a privileged caste. 'The party makes the class,' as the Yugoslav dissident Milovan Djilas argued in 1957, and 'the class grows stronger while the party grows weaker'.

As the historian of ideas George Watson has remarked in *The Lost Literature of Socialism*:

Socialism necessarily means government by a privileged class, as Lenin saw, since only those of privileged education are capable of planning and governing. Shaw and Wells, too, often derided the notion that ordinary people can be trusted with political choice. Hence the aristocratic superiority of the Bolsheviks, who reminded Bertrand Russell, when he visited Lenin soon after the October Revolution, of the British public-school elite that then governed India. Socialism had to be based on privilege, and knew it, since only privilege educates for the due exercise of centralized power in a planned economy.

Marxism displaces one establishment-preserved revealed truth (class, aristocracy, the Old Establishment) with another. But the principle is the same. The Marxists were high priests of received wisdom. We have got the truth, they said, and it is locked in our tabernacle that we drag around. No matter, far from helping us, that it is a clunking burden to progress.

Thus the revolution reinstates that which it despised. In fact, what made Josh fix the engine was not the fact that he was poor and black – though James obviously would not have told the story had he been rich and white. He fixed it because he had been free to think outside the prescriptive limitations of the establishment. A static ruling establishment of Josh Rudders, no matter what their ideals when they began, cannot end up much better than the lazy Scotsmen they replaced.

Beneath the Marxist veneer, James's book is actually a tribute to liberal progress. It celebrates the irrepressible ingenuity of humanity, no matter what the prejudices and challenges it faces. But that was too radical for James to imagine. As Bertolt Brecht was to say, as a Soviet supporter, 'Communism is not radical, capitalism is radical.' James had been brought up in the public-school system, which he rebelled against and eventually utterly rejected. But it had defined him so much that he couldn't see beyond it as a model.

Throughout *Beyond a Boundary*, James refers to W. M. Thackeray's *Vanity Fair* as a huge influence on his intellectual development.

It was not to me an ordinary book. It was a refuge into which I withdrew. By the time I was fourteen I must have read the book over twenty times and I used to confound boys at school telling them to open it anywhere, read a few words, and I would finish the passage, if not the exact words at least close enough . . . I laughed without satiety at Thackeray's constant jokes and sneers at the aristocracy and at people in high places. Thackeray, not Marx, bears the heaviest responsibility.

Indeed he did. But had James examined Thackeray more closely, he would have found some useful, even salutary, warnings. Thackeray was a satirist, but not a real social reformer. His anti-elitism was partly derived from bitterness – the anger of the man standing outside the party with a notebook and pen – and partly from intellectual mischievousness.

When worldly success came to Thackeray, and it came soon enough, he confounded his radical friends by cheerily accepting invitations to sit in the expensive seats with the society figures he had previously satirized. He may have written that the doors of society were so jealously guarded because nothing lay behind them. But in the game of real life, when the door was ajar, he couldn't resist bursting into the room and checking for himself just in case.

In truth, Thackeray had always been in love with society. Otherwise, he could never have described it so accurately and memorably. Like a jilted lover, he learnt by heart society's every flaw and detail – none of which, of course, in any way diminishes the timeless truths of *Vanity Fair*, even if they tell a different story.

James's book, too, is full of truth. But much of it is shoehorned into a false system of thought. He mistakenly believed that *Beyond a Boundary* demonstrated his Marxist ideals. In fact, the history of West Indies cricket disproves them. The book, as is often the case, was wiser than the man.

'Never trust the teller,' said D. H. Lawrence. 'Trust the tale.'

Further reading

Chapter 1

Andrew Berry, 'The Olympic Pool Gene', *Slate* magazine, 5 July 1996
Stephen Jay Gould, *Triumph and Tragedy in Mudville: A Lifelong Passion for Baseball*, Norton, 2003
Steve Jones, *The Single Helix*, Little, Brown, 2005

Chapter 2

Bob Dylan, *Chronicles: Volume One*, Simon & Schuster, 2004; Pocket Books, 2005
Christopher Ricks, *Dylan's Visions of Sin*, Viking, 2003; Penguin, 2004
D. J. Taylor, *On the Corinthian Spirit*, Yellow Jersey Press, 2006

Chapter 3

Anthony Storr, *Feet of Clay: Saints, Sinners and Madmen*, Free Press, 1996; HarperCollins, 1997

Chapter 4

Greg Chappell, *Chappell on Coaching*, Aurum Press, 2005
Michael Lewis, *Moneyball: The Art of Winning an Unfair Game*, Norton, 2003
Steve Waugh, *Out of My Comfort Zone*, Michael Joseph, 2006; Penguin, 2007

Chapter 5

Derek Birley, *A Social History of English Cricket*, Aurum Press, 1999

David Block, *Baseball Before We Knew It: A Search for the Roots of the Game*, University of Nebraska Press, 2005; Bison Books, 2006

Ken Burns and Geoffrey C. Ward, *Baseball*, Alfred A. Knopf, 1994

Richard Cashman and Michael McKernan (eds.), *Sport in History*, University of Queensland Press, 1979

Franklin Foer, *How Football Explains the World*, HarperCollins, 2004; Arrow, 2006

David Goldblatt, *The Ball is Round*, Viking, 2006; Penguin, 2007

Ashis Nandy, *The Tao of Cricket*, OUP India, 2000

Gianluca Vialli and Gabriele Marcotti, *The Italian Job*, Bantam Press, 2006

Chapter 6

Niall Ferguson, *Virtual History: Alternatives and Counterfactuals*, Picador, 1997; Pan, 2003

Duncan Fletcher, *Ashes Regained: The Coach's Story*, Simon & Schuster, 2005; Pocket Books, 2006

Johan Huizinga, 'The Idea of History', reprinted in Fritz Stern, *The Varieties of History: From Voltaire to the Present Day*, Random House, 1988

Chapter 7

David Berry, Martin Schmidt and Stacey Brook, *The Wages of Wins: Taking Measure of the Many Myths in Sport*, Stanford University Press, 2006

Gideon Haigh, *Silent Revolutions: Writings on Cricket History*, Schwartz, 2006; Aurum Press, 2007

Michael Lewis, *The Blind Side: Evolution of a Game*, Norton, 2006

Michael Lewis, *Moneyball: the Art of Winning an Unfair Game*, Norton, 2003

Chapter 8

H. W. Brock, *Game Theory, Social Choice and Ethics*, Kluwer, 1979
Helmut Schoek, *Envy: A Theory of Social Behaviour*, Irvington, 1966;
 new edn, Liberty Fund Inc., 1987
John Wesson, *The Science of Soccer*, Institute of Physics Publishing, 2002

Chapter 9

Renée Fleming, *The Inner Voice: Notes from a Life on Stage*, Virgin,
 2005
Jackie Stewart, *Winning Is Not Enough*, Headline, 2007
Anthony Storr, *Solitude: A Return to the Self*, Free Press, 1988;
 Flamingo, 1997

Chapter 12

Michael Brearley, 'Teams: Lessons from the World of Sport', *British
 Medical Journal*, 4 November 2000

Chapter 15

C. L. R. James, *Beyond a Boundary*, new edn, Yellow Jersey Press,
 2005
George Watson, *The Lost Literature of Socialism*, Lutterworth Press,
 1998

Index of names

He just wanted a decent book to read ...

Not too much to ask, is it? It was in 1935 when Allen Lane, Managing Director of Bodley Head Publishers, stood on a platform at Exeter railway station looking for something good to read on his journey back to London. His choice was limited to popular magazines and poor-quality paperbacks – the same choice faced every day by the vast majority of readers, few of whom could afford hardbacks. Lane's disappointment and subsequent anger at the range of books generally available led him to found a company – and change the world.

'We believed in the existence in this country of a vast reading public for intelligent books at a low price, and staked everything on it'
Sir Allen Lane, 1902–1970, founder of Penguin Books

The quality paperback had arrived – and not just in bookshops. Lane was adamant that his Penguins should appear in chain stores and tobacconists, and should cost no more than a packet of cigarettes.

Reading habits (and cigarette prices) have changed since 1935, but Penguin still believes in publishing the best books for everybody to enjoy. We still believe that good design costs no more than bad design, and we still believe that quality books published passionately and responsibly make the world a better place.

So wherever you see the little bird – whether it's on a piece of prize-winning literary fiction or a celebrity autobiography, political tour de force or historical masterpiece, a serial-killer thriller, reference book, world classic or a piece of pure escapism – you can bet that it represents the very best that the genre has to offer.

Whatever you like to read – trust Penguin.